modern publicity

1977

D1706333

modern publicity

1977

Editor Felix Gluck

VAN NOSTRAND REINHOLD COMPANY
NEW YORK   CINCINNATI   TORONTO   LONDON   MELBOURNE

The new typeface designs shown on pages 81, 82, 83, 84 and 85 are copyright of the type foundries, designers or photosetting companies. They must not be used without the permission of the copyright holders or their licensees.

Copyright © 1977 by
Studio Vista, a division of Cassell & Collier Macmillan
Publishers Limited.

Library of Congress Catalog Card Number 76-29540
ISBN 0-442-22707-8

All rights reserved. No part of this work covered by the copyright
hereon may be reproduced or used in any form or by any means — graphic,
electronic, or mechanical, including photocopying, recording, taping,
or information storage and retrieval systems — without written permission
of the publisher.

Printed in Great Britain.

Published in 1977 by Van Nostrand Reinhold Company
A division of Litton Educational Publishing, Inc.
450 West 33rd Street, New York, NY 10001, U.S.A.

Van Nostrand Reinhold Limited
1410 Birchmount Road
Scarborough, Ontario M1P 2E7, Canada

16 15 14 13 12 11 10 9 8 7 6 5 4 3 2 1

Contents

Sommaire

Inhalt

The cover design chosen for this year's *Modern Publicity* is based on a poster designed by Bruno Scarton for the Swiss Telephone authorities. The idea of painting objects before they are photographed is not so new, but by using the various national colours on the telephones a simple message for the use of direct dialling is conveyed forcefully and effectively.

This year's most impressive coordinated campaigns by multinational corporations came from the Olivetti Studios who are equally successful in their posters, advertisements and direct mail material.

In the poster section Per Nagel's Citroen 2CV poster is a delightful selection of photographs in a straightforward design presentation. The poster is really an advertisement for the photographer, who uses the popularity of the 2CV and his own ingenuity in finding the extravagant examples and photographing them, as a means to find new clients.

The Swissair West Africa poster is again a straight photograph, remarkable in its crispness. No wonder Gerster's book of aerial photography is the publishing success of the year.

In the press advertisement section the advertisement on page 76 for Chivers marmalade and the Wedgwood advertisement on the same page have a certain similarity of approach in the way they manipulate the objects most competently to present the art directors' almost surrealist ideas.

In the bookjacket sections the Norske Bokklubben is outstanding for the elegance of its typography, lay-out, binding and bookjackets for a popular market.

In the postage stamp section we grouped a number of subjects to give our readers a chance to see how designers in various countries found different solutions to the same problem.
The US Bicentenary was celebrated in many countries by the issue of postage stamps. Some states used a similar technique to that of the US postal administration, who perforated the reproduction of a painting into separate stamps. Others gave their designers a free hand and the variety is very interesting.

International Women's Year was another occasion which was celebrated all over the world by special stamps being issued. It is interesting to note that very few women were commissioned to design the stamps propagating the equality of women. The Olympic Games and Bell's telephone anniversary provided us with a further basis for the comparison of the work of individual designers whose countries submitted their stamp designs. We had to find and select additional stamps to extend the variety of material in this section and hope that in the future more designers will submit their postage stamp designs personally.

In the packaging section the soap package designs for Crabtree and Evelyn are most attractive; they combine nostalgia with modern taste and an individuality in design. Ferenc Pinter's humorous wrapping paper for Mondadori shows the variety of the publisher's booklist through cartoons of the various characters, ie crime, romance, science-fiction etc.

In the letterhead section the stationery for Grey's advertising is most impressive not only for its style in design, but also for the way in which the entire progress of a job is recorded in a variety of easy, comprehensible and attractive forms, which must be a pleasure for staff and clients to fill in.

In TV advertising the Wyatt Cattaneo Studios and Nationale Publiciteits Onderneming provide some of the most successful commercials, in animated cartoons. It would be useful if our contributors would send in the text with their TV commercial material as it is difficult to show sequences of still photographs without the text — which is usually important.

In the direct mail section Zanders have yet again produced original ways of publicising their papers. Their ingenious cut-outs prove that there are still more and more avenues to explore and that lively art direction and inventive designers can create new and striking results. One year is not a very long period to detect new trends or developments in design, even if the year is stretched longer, as happened for technical reasons with this edition of our book. In general one finds that designers and copywriters are more aware of the demand for the credibility of their claims. But in style little has changed over the past year.

I would like to thank our contributors, agencies, clients and art directors, who have submitted their work for this issue, and hope that they will send their new work again as usual and that they will not have been discouraged if none of their work has been published in this present issue of *Modern Publicity*.

Felix Gluck

Introduction

La couverture de l'édition de *Modern Publicity* de cette année est basée sur une affiche de Bruno Scarton pour la Compagnie de Téléphone Suisse. L'idée de peindre les objets avant de les photographier n'est pas nouvelle, mais l'emploi des couleurs nationales sur les appareils de téléphone transmet de façon très frappante un message simple pour l'emploi du téléphone automatique internationale.

Les plus remarquables campagnes internationales de l'année viennent des Studios Olivetti, qui ont autant de succès avec leurs affiches qu'avec leurs annonces et leurs brochures.

Dans le chapitre des Affiches, celle de Per Nagel pour la Citroën 2 CV donne une sélection de photos charmantes avec une présentation assez directe. Cette affiche est une réclame pour le photographe, qui emploie la popularité des Deux Chevaux et sa propre ingéniosité pour les photographier afin de trouver des nouveaux clients.

L'affiche de Swissair avec une photo de Georg Gerster est remarquable par sa netteté d'exécution. Il n'est pas étonnant que le livre de photos aeriennes de Gerster soit un des grands succès de cette année.

Dans le chapitre des Annonces de Presse les réclames pour la marmelade Chivers et l'idée pour la vaisselle de Wedgwood allant au four furent toutes les deux fort efficaces dans leur genre. Il est intéressant de voir comme les objets furent manipulés intelligemment, de façon à présenter aux directeurs artistiques des idées presque surrealistes sur les photos.

Dans le chapitre sur Chemises de Livres, les dessins pour le Norske Bokklubben sont remarquables. Il est parvenu à donner à ce club de livres populaires une qualité de dessin, une élégance de typographie, de reliure et de chemises de livres que c'est un vrai plaisir de manier tous leurs livres.

Dans le chapitre sur les Timbres de Poste, nous groupons un nombre de projets pour donner à nos lecteurs la chance de voir comment les dessinateurs ont réalisé le même sujet dans différents pays.

On a célébré universellement avec des timbres de poste le bi-centenaire des E.U. Certains pays ont employé une technique semblable à celle de l'administration des E.U. en divisant un tableu pour en faire des timbres séparés. D'autres ont laissé l'initiative à leurs dessinateurs; de ce fait le résultat est varié et très intéressant.

L'Année Internationale de la Femme fut une autre occasion de publier partout des timbres pour célébrer cet évènement. Il est intéressant de noter qu'on a demandé à peu de femmes de créer des timbres pour propager l'idée de l'égalité de la femme.

Les Jeux Olympiques et l'anniversaire du Téléphone Bell nous a donné une autre occasion d'analyser et de comparer le travail de divers dessinateurs dans les pays qui soumirent leurs timbres.

Nous avons dû trouver et sélectionner des timbres supplémentaires pour donner plus de variété au matériel de ce chapitre, et nous espérons que, lorsque cette section sera mieux connue, les dessinateurs ne laisseront pas le choix des timbres seulement aux Directeurs des Postes, mais qu'ils enverront aussi eux-memes leurs dessins.

Dans le chapitre sur les Emballages les emballages de savon de Crabtree sont très attrayants; les dessins allient une atmosphère nostalgique au goût moderne et individuel. Les papiers d'emballage très humoristiques de Ferenc Pinter pour Mondadori montrent la grande variété de leur liste de livres pour des sujets divers, par example, crime, science, roman etc. La même idée a été employée pour leurs affiches.

Dans le chapitre sur les En-Têtes j'aimerais louer spécialement celles du studio de publicité Grey, faites pour leur propre agence. Cette série est remarquable, non seulement par le style du dessin, mais aussi par la façon dont toute la progression d'un travail est montrée sur des formulaires attrayants, faciles à comprendre, que le personnel et les clients doivent avoir grand plaisir à remplir (et c'est une chose en général bien difficile à accomplir!)

Dans le chapitre de Réclames de T.V. le studio Wyatt-Cattaneo et Nationale Publiciteits Onderneming donnent le matériel le plus humoristique, et la B.B.C. nous a envoyé des titres de programmes de très grande qualité, employant l'animation photographique de façon remarquable.

Finalement nous arrivons au chapitre des Brochures, où Olaf Leu et son studio ont une fois de plus montré des façons originales de présenter du papier pour Zander. Leurs découpages des Radiateurs Rolls-Royce prouvent qu'il y a encore beaucoup de chemins à explorer, et que des dessinateurs inventifs peuvent créer de nouveaux résultats frappants, même si cela ne signifie pas une tendance nouvelle dans le dessin en une seule année. Une année n'est pas une très longue période dans le développement ou les tendances du dessin, même si elle se prolonge un peu, comme cela s'est passé pour raisons techniques dans cette édition de Modern Publicity. Nous nous excusons de ce délai de publication, et espérons publier la prochaine édition à la date habituelle.

J'aimerais remercier nos collaborateurs, agences, clients et directeurs artistiques, qui ont présenté leurs travaux pour cette édition, et espérons qu'ils continueront à nous les envoyer comme par le passé, sans se décourager si, par manque de place, leur ouvrage n'a pas paru dans cette édition.

Felix Gluck

Der Umschlagsentwurf für *Modern Publicity* beruht dieses Jahr auf einem Plakat für die schweizerische Telephondirektion das von Bruno Scarton entworfen wurde. Im Grunde genommen, ist die Methode die Objekte vor dem photographieren zu malen, nicht sehr neu. Die Verwendung der verschiedenen Nationalfarben auf den Telephonhörern bringt aber die Idee des Direktwählens im internationalen Telephonverkehr mit einfachen und effektiven Mitteln zum Ausdruck.

Die eindrucksvollste ko-ordinierte Kampagne internationaler Gesellschaften kam dieses Jahr von Olivetti, das Niveau der Plakate, Inserate und Broschuren war einheitlich hoch.

In der Plakat-sektion wählten wir Per Nagel's Citroen 2CV Plakat als Öffnungsseite. Es ist eine einfache grafische Lösung zur Präsentation einer wunderbaren Auswahl von Photos exzentrischer 2CV Wagen. Das Plakat is allerdings eine Reklame für den Photographen, der die Volkstümlichkeit des 2CV Autos und sein photographisches Talent kombiniert um neue Auftraggeber zu finden.

Das Swissair-West-Afrika Plakat ist wiederum eine einfache grafische Lösung aber die Schärfe des Luftphotos verdient besonders erwähnt zu werden. Es ist verständlich, dass Gerster's Flug-photobuch der grosse Verlagserfolg des Jahres war.

Im Inseratenteil finden wir viele originelle photografische Lösungen wie z.B. die Inserate für Chivers Marmelade und die Wedgwood Porzellantöpfe, die im Grundkonzept eine gewisse Ähnlichkeit haben. Beide Inserate haben ihre Wirksamkeit denjenigen zu danken, die die fast surrealistischen Ideen der Art-Direktors so genau und kompetent dargestellt haben. In unserem Kapitel für Buchumschläge möchte ich besonders den Norske Bokklubben erwähnen. Das Niveau und die Eleganz der Typographie, des Lay-outs der Einbände und der Umschläge ist hervorragend.

Im Kapitel für Briefmarkenentwürfe gruppierten wir einen Teil des Materials nach Thematik, um unseren Lesern die Möglichkeit zu geben, zu vergleichen, wie Grafiker in verschiedenen Ländern das gleiche Problem gelöst haben.

Die USA Zweihundert-Jahr-Feier wurde zum Beispiel überall mit Sondermarken begrüsst. Einige Länder verwendeten die neue Technik der Postdirektion der Vereinigten Staaten die eine Gemäldereproduktion perforierte, andere Länder gaben ihren Entwerfern freie Hand und die verschiedenen Lösungen sind interessant (z.B. die Irischen Marken auf Seite 97). Das Jahr der Frau gab uns eine andere Vergleichsmöglichkeit. Es war aber interessant zu bemerken wie wenige Frauen beauftragt wurden diese Sondermarken für die Gleichberechtigung der Frau zu entwerfen.
Wir mussten weitere Briefmarken zur Erweiterung unserer Auswahl finden und hoffen dass in der Zukunft neben den Postdirektionen die zwar hilfsbereit sind, aber in ihren Einsendungen eine Vorwahl machen, auch die Grafiker selbst ihre neuen Markentwürfe einsenden werden.

Im Verpackungskapitel waren die Seifenverpackungen für Crabtree und Evelyn sehr attraktiv. Die Nostalgie wurde hier mit moderner Eleganz verbunden.

Ferenc Pintérs humorvolle Packpapiere für Mondadori publizierten geistreich eine weite Liste von Büchern dieses Verlages durch Karrikaturen der verschiedenen Titel wie z.B. Kriminalromane, Liebesromane, Science-Fiction, usw.

Die Briefköpfe für Grey's Advertising sind nicht nur als grafische Lösung eindrucksvoll, sondern auch wegen der Art und Weise in der die Formulare ausgedacht sind, um den Fortschritt eines Projektes zu dokumentieren. Es muss wirklich vergnüglich sein diese Formulare auszufüllen.

In TV Reklame sind Wyatt-Cattaneo's und Nationale Publiciteits Onderneming am lebhaftesten. Wir würden gerne mehr Material in diesem Kapitel zeigen und hoffen dass unsere Einsender uns mehr TV und Film-Reklame senden. Es ist aber schwierig Film Auszüge zu zeigen wenn wir nicht Begleittexte haben die die Szenen erklären.

In der Direkt-Mail Sektion, haben Zanders Papierfabriken wiederum neue Ideen und Möglichkeiten zur Reklame gefunden. Die Idee der gestanzten Illustrationen und deren Hintergrund wurde auch technisch ausgezeichnet durchgeführt und beweist dass es immer neuere Möglichkeiten gibt dasselbe Thema zu behandeln. Lebendige Art-Direction und erfinderische Entwerfer beweisen dass man auch weiterhin überraschende und amüsante Lösungen finden kann.

Ein Jahr ist nicht sehr lange um neue Entwicklungen und Trends zu spüren und zu beurteilen, auch dann nicht wenn das Jahr aus technischen Grunden wie bei dieser Auflage zu 15 Monaten wurde. Aber im Entwurfsstil hat sich trotzdem nicht viel verändert.

Ich danke wiederum allen Grafikern, Werbeagenturen, Teams und Firmen, die mit Ihren Einsendungen zu der Vielfältigkeit dieses Buches beigetragen haben und ich hoffe dass auch jene wiederum Material einsenden werden, deren Arbeiten wir dieses Jahr nicht zeigen konnten.

Felix Gluck

INDEX

INDEX

INDEX

Artists, designers photographers, producers and art directors

Advertising agents, and studios

Agences et studios

CITROËN★2CV

1

2a-b

4

5

Abbreviations
Abkürzungen

AD Advertiser
    Client
    Auftraggeber

AG Agency/Studio
    Agence/Atelier
    Reklameberater

DIR Art director
    Directeur artistique
    Künstlerischer Leiter

DES Designer/Artist
    Maquettiste/Artiste
    Grafiker/Künstler

ILL Illustrator/Photographer

Posters

Affiches

Plakate

1 Denmark
AD/DES Per Nagel
Citroen cars and self promotion,
auto-promotion

3

この世界に一着しかないジーンズを作らないか。最愛のジーンズにひと腕ふるって。作品募集中

リーバイス・デニムアート・コンテスト

Posters
Affiches
Plakate

1 Great Britain
AD Barclays Bank Ltd
AG Barclays Bank Advertising Department
DIR/DES John York
bank

2a-b Canada
AD/AG Cooper & Beatty Ltd
DIR/DES James Donoahue
ILL Ray Webber—Format
agency-promotion

3 Japan
AD Levi Strauss (Far East) Ltd
AG Interpublic—Hakuhodo
DIR Tateo Ikunaga
DES Kunimasa Hatachi
ILL Eirchiro Sakata
jeans

4 Japan
AD Isuzu Motors
AG McCann Erickson-Hakuhodo
DIR Mitsuhiko Sasao
DES Katsuhiro Takemura
ILL GM Photographer Group
COPY Joji Kashu
car, auto

5 Canada
AD Graphic Litho-Plate Ltd
AG Burns & Cooper Ltd
DIR/DES James Donoahue
ILL Photographics
colour separation

6

6 Japan
AD Levi Strauss (Far East) Ltd
AG Interpublic-Hakuhodo
DIR Tateo Ikunaga
DES Kunimasa Hatachi
ILL Kaoni Ueda
COPY Koichi Hara
jeans

18-19

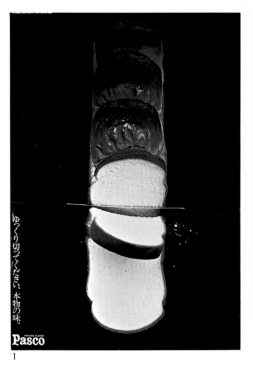

1

2

3

5

6

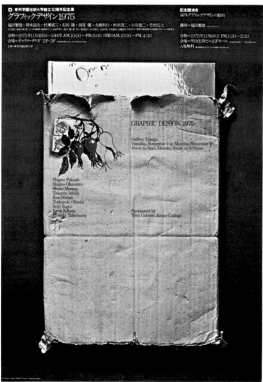

4a–b

1 Japan
AD Shikishima Baking Co. Ltd
AG Shigeo Okamoto Design Center
DIR Shigeo Okamoto
ILL Toshiyuki Ohashi
bread, pain, Brot

2 United States
AD Colorado State University
AG Bob Coonts Graphic Design
DES Bob Coonts
summer course

3 Italy
AD Council of Europe
AG Associazione Italiana per il World
      Wild Life Fund
DIR Fulco Pratesi

4a-b Japan
AD (a) Tohogakuen Junior College,
      (b) Shikishima Baking Co. Ltd
AG Shigeo Okamoto Design Center
DIR/DES Shigeo Okamoto
ILL (a) Toshiyuki Ohashi, (b) Shigeo Okamoto
(a) exhibition
(b) Christmas poster

5 Germany
AD Bayerischer Rundfunk
DES Walter Tafelmaier
ILL Michael Tafelmaier
radio, television

6 Japan
AD Meitetsu Melsa
AG Shigeo Okamoto Design Center
DIR Ken Nishio, Shigeo Okamoto
DES Shigeo Okamoto
ILL Toshiyuki Ohashi
COPY Ken Nishio
exhibition

7 Japan
AD Tohogakuen Junior College
AG Shigeo Okamoto Design Center
DIR/DES Shigeo Okamoto
ILL Toshiyuki Ohashi
COPY Ken Nishio
Christmas poster

7

白夜への郷愁

Christmas
& New year
Fashion
1975–76
Sakae
Melsa

20-21

1

2

3

5

6

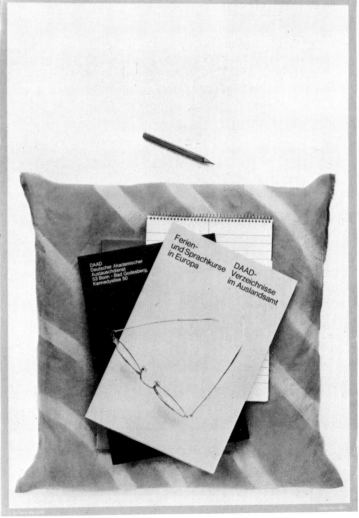

4

7

1 Italy
AD Itres, Nera Montoro
AG Studioelle
DIR/DES Ennio Lucini
windows, fenêtres, Fenster

2 Japan
AD Olivetti Corporation of Japan
AG PAC Division, Olivetti Corporation of Japan
DIR Tetsro Itoh
DES Tadaaki Kanasashi
ILL Hiromi Tomita
portable typewriter, machine à écrire
    Schreibmaschine

3 Italy
AD Olivetti Suisse S.A.
AG Ufficio Pubblicita Olivetti—S.P.P.
DIR/DES Giovanni Ferioli
office machines

4 Italy
AD Ing. C. Olivetti & C., S.p.A.
AG Ufficio Design e Grafica Pubblicitaria
office machines

5 Germany
AD Edeka
DES Heno Petersen
honey, miel, Honig

6 Germany
AD Deutscher Akademischer Austauschdienst
DES Heinz Bähr
holiday and language courses in Europe, cours
de vacances et de langues en Europe,
Ferien- und Sprachkurse in Europa

7 Argentina
AD IKA Renault
DES Segundo Freire
motorcars, autos

1

2

3

5

6

4

7

1 Italy
AD Seggiano Cheese
AG Promos
DIR Brian Murrels
ILL Carlo Facchini
cheese, fromage, Jäse

2 Israel
AD Maskit Ltd
DES Ruth Lubin
craft shop

3 Czechoslovakia
AD Biennale of Illustrations
ILL M. Vesely, J. Novy
exhibition

4 United States
AD Student Services Inc.
AG Gauger Sparks Silva
DIR/DES David Gauger
summer jobs programme for students

5 United States
AD ASMP SO Cal Chapter
AG The Weller Institute
DIR/DES Don Weller, Chikako Matsubayashi
ILL Marv Lyons
COPY Tom Groener

6 Great Britain
AD Penguin Books
DES Malcolm Hawdon
cookery books

7 Canada
AD/AG Burns & Cooper
DIR/DES Heather Cooper
'The Art of the Illustrator' — exhibition

1

2a–b

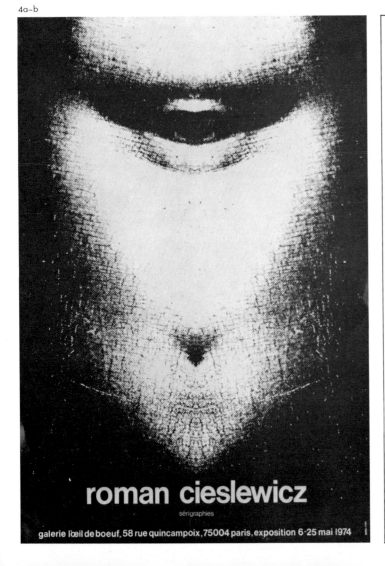

4a–b

roman cieslewicz

sérigraphies

galerie l'œil de boeuf, 58 rue quincampoix, 75004 paris, exposition 6-25 mai 1974

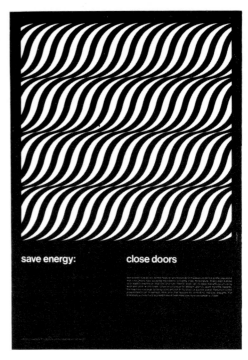

théâtre
d'angers

serigraphies
en noir et blanc

entrée libre

exposition

exposition
ouverte
du 4 décembre
1975
au 18 janvier
1976
tous les jours sauf lundi
de 15 h à 19 h

roman cieslewicz

1 Germany
AD Staatliche Museen Berlin
DES Jürgen Spohn
museums

2a-b Great Britain
AD Leeds University/Polytechnic
AG De Morgan Associates
DIR/DES Jonathan de Morgan
COPY Jonathan de Morgan, David Morris
save energy campaign, campagne pour
    ménager l'énergie

3 Great Britain
AD Public Relations Group, Post
    Office—Northern Region
DES Laszlo Ács
economic use of fuels, usage économique de
    combustibles, Heizmaterial sparen

4a-b France
AD (a) Galerie l'Oeil de Boeuf, (b) Theatre
    Municipal d'Angers
DIR (b) Daniel Chomprée
AG/DES Roman Cièslewícz
exhibition

5 Germany
AD Haus am Waldsee
DES Jürgen Spohn
ILL Iris Papadopoulos
poetry reading, récital de poésie, Lesung

6 United States
AD Student Services West
AG Gauger Sparks Silva
DIR/DES David Gauger, Walter Sparks
student travel, voyages d'étudiants, Studenten
    Reisen

3

5

6

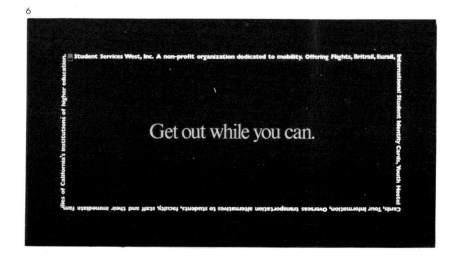

materialbilder
tegninger
skisser
grafikk
forsider
bokutstyr
for
over
300
bøker
Hans
Jørgen
Toming
stiller
ut
i
Moss
Kunstgalleri
i
tiden
6. januar
til
22. januar

1

2

Vår tids scenebilde
Henie Onstad
Kunstsenter Høvik-
odden 17. april–6. juni

4

8 март

5

6

3

28-29

Rosenmontagsball

Bühne
Presse
Feuerio

1

Bonduelle ist das famose
Zartgemüse aus der Dose

2a

**Er heizt das Haus und liefert auch
viel Wasser für den Hausgebrauch.
Der Bitherm GPM**

Der Universal-Gaskessel mit Warmwasser-
Bereitung von Ideal-Standard.
Mit der Technik der besseren Energieausnutzung.
Mit der Form fürs schönere Heizen.

IDEAL STANDARD

2b

2c

**DAS HAUS bringt mehr Coupon-Rücklauf,
denn jede Schere stürzt sich drauf.**

Die besten Kontakte sind Aktiv-Kontakte

2d

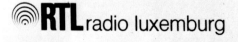

RTL radio luxemburg

3

1 Germany
AD Karnevalsverein, Mannheim
DES Wolf Magin
carneval

2a-d Germany
AD (a) Bonduelle S.A.,
  (b) Ideal Standard GmbH,
  (c) Burda Verlag,
  (d) Radio Luxemburg
AG Werbeagentur Robert Pütz GmbH & Co
DIR Robert Pütz
ILL Tomi Ungerer
COPY Adolf Limbach
(a) canned vegetables, boites de legume,
  Gemüse Konserven
(b) boiler, chaudière, Heizkessel
(c) magazines, hebdomadaires, Zeitschriften
(d) radio

3 Germany (DDR)
AD Künstler Agentur der DDR
DES Feliks Büttner
marionette theatre, theatre de marionetts,
  Puppentheater

4a-b Denmark
AD Burmeister & Wain AS
AG Scherling & Andersen AS
DIR/DES Johnny Lund
against abuse of electricity, contre l'abus de
  l'éléctricité, Stromsparen

4 a–b

1a

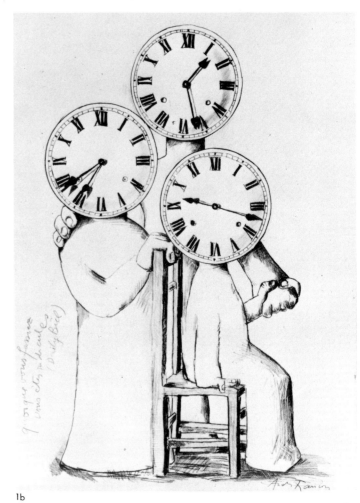

1b

1c

2

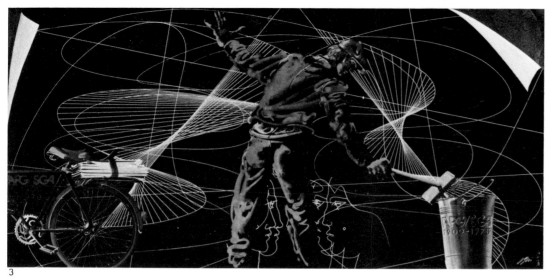

3

1a-c France
AD (a,b) Daily Búl
   (c) SNCF
DES André François
(a,b) publication
(c) French Railways

2 Germany
AD Kunstfreunde Rostock
DES Feliks Büttner
Friends of Art, Les amis de l'art

3 Switzerland
AD Ministry of Labour
DES Hans Erni
trade unions, syndicats

4a-b Sweden
AD/AG Svenske Naturskyddsforeningen
DES Erik Brunn

4a–b

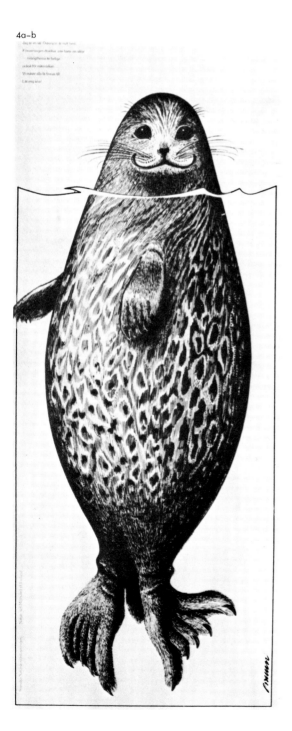

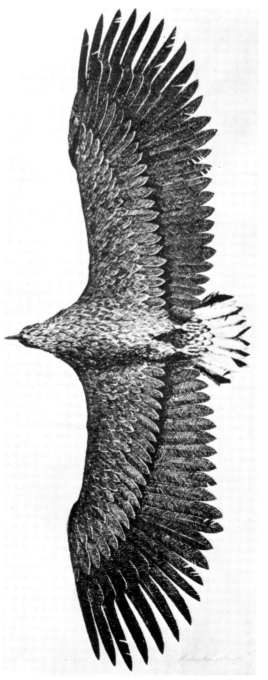

Kapitelle und Säulen

Kirchliche Gegenstände und Klösterliche Räume

Braunschweigisches Landesmuseum für Geschichte und Volkstum
Hinter Aegidien Lessingplatz Telefon 05 31/4 84 919

Ständige Ausstellungen in historischen Räumen
Geöffnet Di-Mi Do-Sa 10-17 Fr 10-16 So 10-13 Uhr Montags geschlossen

Landesmuseum
an der Aegidienkirche

1 a–b

4

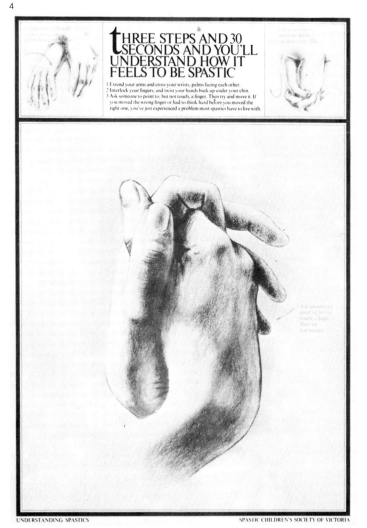

5

2

3

6

1

2a–b

Am Brunnen vor dem Tore
von Franz Schubert
High Fidelity von Wega
WEGA

Der Zigeunerbaron
von Johann Strauß
High Fidelity von Wega

4

5

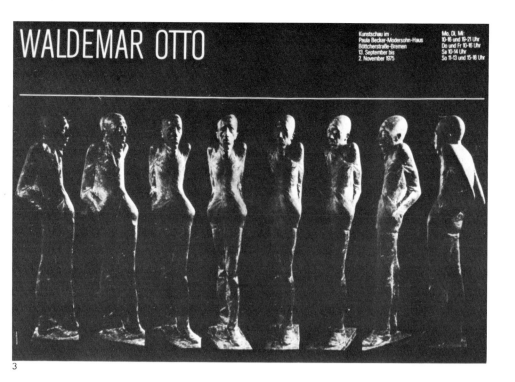

3

6

Posters
Affiches
Plakate

1 United States
AD C.S.U. Music Department
AG C.S.U. Art Department
DIR/DES Phil Risbeck
opera

2a-b Switzerland
AD Wega-Radio GmbH
AG Leonhardt & Kern
DIR G. Leonhardt
DES Hans-Peter Kamm
ILL Ernst Wirz
hi-fi

3 Germany
AD Waldemar Otto, sculptor
DES Reinhart Braun
exhibition

4 France
AD C.C.I.
AG Grapus
exhibition

5 Czechoslovakia
DES Jaroslav Sura
Music Festival

6 Germany
AD 'Aktionsgemeinschaft Solidarische Welt'
DES Reinhart Braun
ILL Harry Suchland
for 'World in Solidarity', pour la solidarité
mondiale, für Weltsolidarität

1 a–b

2

5

4 b

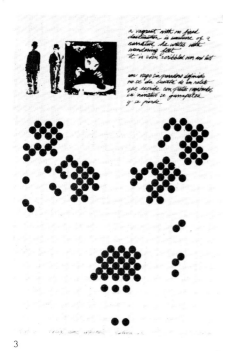

3

4a

1a-b Switzerland
AD Opernhaus Zürich
AG Werbeagentur MB & Co
DIR (a) Ruedi Rüegg,
(b) Peter Spalinger
DES (a) Peter Spalinger,
Barbara Saxer

2 Great Britain
AD Prospect Theatre Company
AG Friends Design Workshop
DIR/DES Clifford Richards
theatre

3 Great Britain
AD Chelsea School of Art
DES Edward Wright
exhibition

4a-b Belgium
AD Théâtre National de Belgique
DIR Manfred Hürrig
DES Manfred Hürrig, Anne Velghe
theatre

5 Israel
AD Mifal hapais — state lottery
AG State Publicity Dept
DIR/DES Asher Kalderon
lottery

6a-b Germany
AD Serie 3X Theatergemeinde Berlin
DES Peter Klemke
theatre

6a

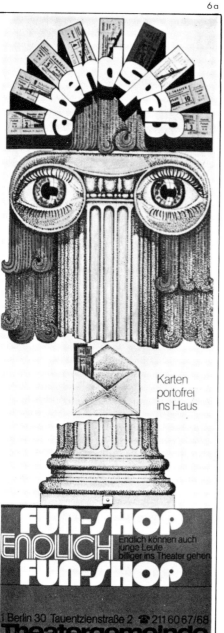

6b

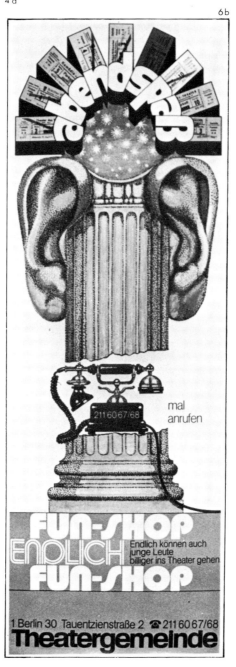

1 Great Britain
AD London Transport
DIR M. F. Levey
DES T. Eckersley
London transport museum

2 Switzerland
AD Publizitätsdienst SBB
AG Publicity Department Swiss Federal
Railways
DIR/DES Dr. Werner Belmont
ILL Philipp Giegel
COPY Peter Farner, Werner Belmont
railways, chemin-de-fer, Eisenbahn

3 Italy
AD Ente Provinciale Turismo Milano
DES K. D. Geissbühler
tourism

4 Poland
AD/AG KAW — Krajowa Agencja Wydawnicza
DIR Gustaw Majewski
DES Jan Mlodozeniec
tourism

5 Switzerland
AD Swissair Propaganda
AG GGK, Basel
tourism

6 Holland
AD Het Nederlands Zuivelbureau
AG Prad B.V.
DIR Mariet Numan
ILL Mariet Numan
COPY Jan Lenferink
tourism

7a-b Italy
AD Fabbriche Accumulatori Riunite SpA
DES Alfredo de Santís
batteries

1

2

6

milano

Wer Mailand
nicht gesehen hat
der kennt Italien nicht!

3

POLAND invites you

4

Mit den Swissair-
Weekendtarifen
bis zu 40% billiger
nach
20 europäischen
Destinationen.

SWISSAIR

Bald ist wieder
Wochenende.

5

7a–b

BATTERIE STAZIONARIE PER EMERGENZA LUCE SUSSIDIARIA SEGNALAMENTO E TELEFONIA

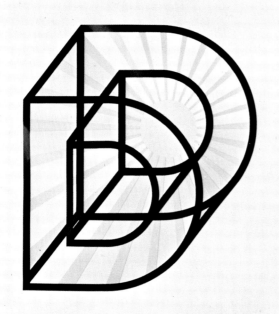

1a

1b

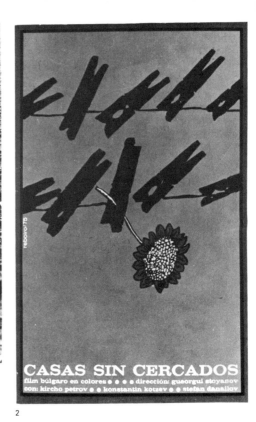

2

5

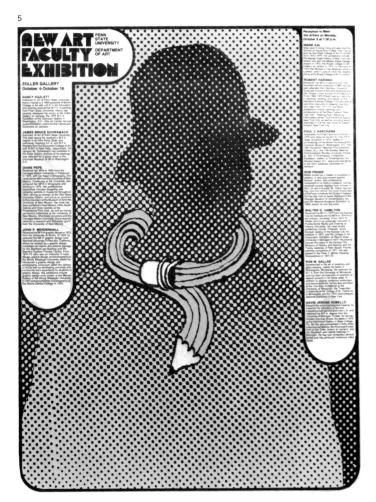

6

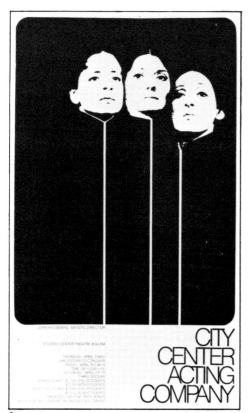

4

3

7

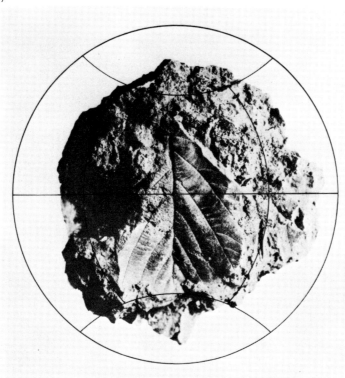

1a-b Germany
AD (a) Süddeutscher Rundfunk Stuttgart
Fernsehen
(b) Staatstheater Darmstadt
DES Frieder Grindler
(a) television, (b) theatre

2 Cuba
AD/AG ICAIC
DES Antonio Fernández Reboiro
filmposter

3 United States
AD C.S.U. Fine Arts Series
AG C.S.U. Art Department
DIR/DES Phil Risbeck
dance company

4 Canada
AD The National Ballet of Canada
AG Raymond Lee & Associates Ltd
DIR/DES Raymond Lee
ILL LTK Production
ballet

5 United States
AD Art Department, Penn State University
AG Lanny Sommese Design
DIR/DES Lanny Sommese
exhibition

6 Czechoslovakia
AD Ústav lidového umení Stráznice
AG Propagacní tvorba
DIR Jan Rajlich
DES Petr Jero
folk art

7 Hungary
AD Magyar Hirdetö
DES Magda Vörösmarty
protection of the environment

Farbig

sind
Hamburgs
Museen

1

Romanisten

Semesterstipendien des DAAD/DFJW für Asnières, Lille, Lyon, Nantes,
Orléans, Poitiers, Reims, Rennes, Toulouse und Tours
im Wintersemester 74/75. Einzelheiten beim Akademischen Auslandsamt
oder Sekretariat. Bewerbungsschluß

30.5.

Ein Plakat des DAAD.   Design Heinz Bähr

2

4

textile ●bjekte

Museum für Kunst und Gewerbe Hamburg
11.9 bis 26.10.   Täglich, ausser montags
10-17 Uhr
10-19 Uhr mittwochs

5

Montréal 1976

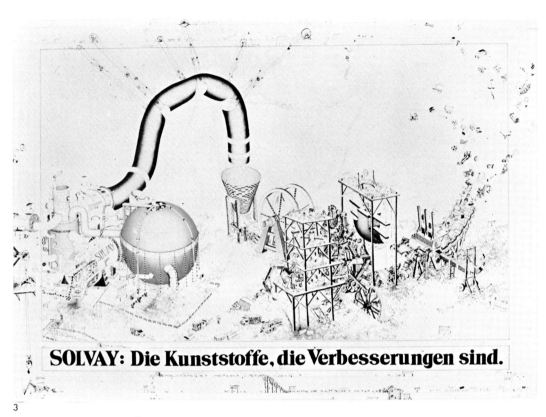

SOLVAY: Die Kunststoffe, die Verbesserungen sind.

3

1 Germany
AD Behörde für Wissenschaft u. Kunst
DES Holger Matthies
museum

2 Germany
AD Deutscher Akademischer Austauschdienst
DES Heinz Bähr
French scholarship, Stipendien

3 Germany
AD Solvay & Cie
AG Robert Pütz
DES Uwe Brandi
PVC, plastics

4 Germany
AD Hamburg Museum
DES Holger Matthies
exhibition

5 Canada
AD Comite Organisateur des Jeux de la XXIe
Olympiade
AG Design Collaborative
DIR/DES Ernst Roch
Olympic Games in Montreal

6 Italy
AD Ing. C. Olivetti & c., S.p.A.
AG Ufficio Design e Grafica Pubblicitaria
DIR Franco Bassi

6

1

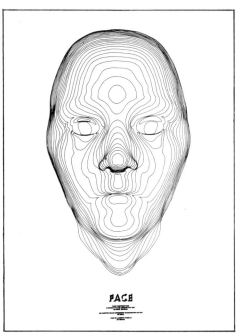

FACE

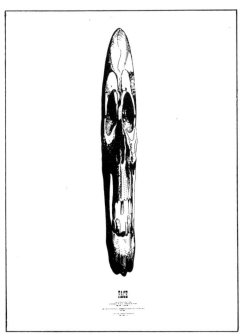

FACE

2a-b

3a-b

rotring

rotring

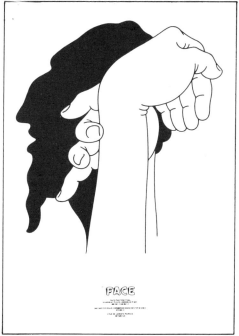

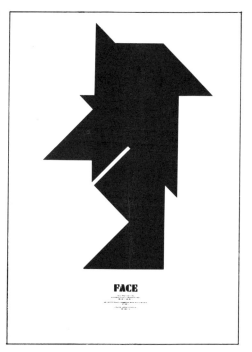

2c-d

1 Canada
AD Ontario College of Art
AG Burns & Cooper Ltd
DIR/DES Robert Burns
ILL Heather Cooper, Paul Walker
lecture by Milton Glaser

2 a-d Great Britain
AD Face Photosetting
AG Pentagram
DIR/DES John McConnell
typefaces, phototypo, Fotosatz

3a-b Great Britain
AD Hartley Reece
AG Pentagram
DIR/DES Mervyn Kurlansky
ILL (a) Peter Cook,
    (b) Milton Glaser
drawing pens for designers

4 Japan
AD RCA Victor Records Company
DES Tadanori Yokoo
records, disques

4

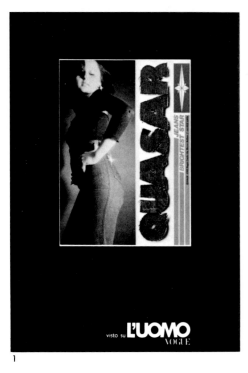

1

2

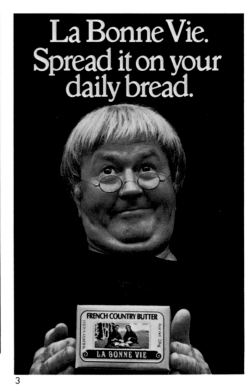

3

5

6

4a–b

1 Italy
AD Quasar Jeans
AG Studio Arletti
DIR/DES Elis Arletti
ILL Ebro Arletti
jeans

2 Belgium
AD Woluwé shopping centre
AG/DES S. & S. Alouf
exhibition

3 Great Britain
AD Aqualac Alimentaire
AG Leo Burnett Ltd
DIR/DES Stewart Howard
ILL Barney Edwards
COPY Ron Bond
butter, beurre

4a-b Canada
AD McGregor Hosiery Mills
AG Raymond Lee & Associates Ltd
DIR/DES Raymond Lee
ILL (a) Viktor von Maderspach,
    (b) Rudi Christl
COPY (a) Leo Bautista,
    (b) Raymond Lee
socks, chaussettes, Socken

5 Switzerland
AD Creation Pommesa
DES K. Domenig Geissbühler
ILL Dave Buhlmann
jeans

6 Holland
AD Louet B.V.
AG Integral Design Unit
DES Jeanne and Robert Schaap
ILL Jeanne Schaap
spinning wheels, rouets, Spinnrad

7 United States
AD Temple University
AG Joe Scorsone
DES Joe Scorsone
DIR William Larson
COPY William Larson
lectures on photography

8 Great Britain
AD National Portrait Gallery
AG HMSO Graphic Design
DIR/DES Christabel Hardacre
exhibition of photographs

7

8

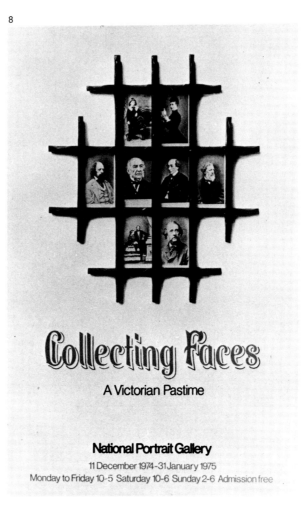

1

IRAN'S FUTURE FILM-MAKERS

2

Local de Inscrição

Fac. Arquitetura/UFPe
Prédio Institutos Básicos 9º Andar
Cidade Universitária/Recife
ou no Escritório Regional
da SUDENE de sua Cidade

Universidade Federal de Pernambuco

MESTRADO EM DESENVOLVIMENTO URBANO

Prazo de Inscrição
13 Jan a 14 Fev/1975

Convênio

UFPe/MEC
MINTER/SEPLAN/SUDENE

3

5

"ALL TOGETHER NOW: HAPPY BIRTHDAY USA"

6

The Useful Willow

Bexley Libraries
& Museums
Service

Saturday 1 March to Monday
31 March
10am-5pm Weekdays
2pm-6pm Sundays from
16 March

An exhibition displaying the
versatility of the willow as
used in basket making.
Hall Place, Bourne Road,
Bexley.

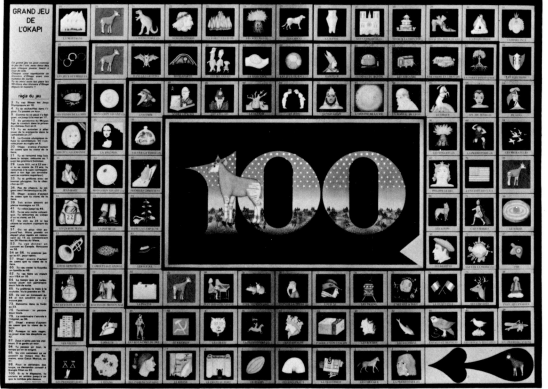

4

7

**Posters
Affiches
Plakate**

1 Iran
AD The Institute for the Intellectual
Development of Children and Young Adults
DES E. Haghighi
children's film

2 Iran
AD Tehran International Film Festival
DES Morteza Momayez
ILL Mohammad Reza Adnani, Ali Khosrari
COPY Hagir Daryoush

3 Brazil
AD Universidade Federal de Pernambuco
AG Cunha Lima e Associados
DIR/DES Guilherme Cunha Lima
ILL Fritz Simons
post-graduate course in urbanism

4 France
AD Okapi magazine
DES Denys Prache
childrens magazine, Kinderzeitschrift

5 United States
AD Davis-Delaney-Arrow, Inc.
AG George Tscherny, Inc.
DIR/DES George Tscherny
U.S. Bicentennial

6 Great Britain
AD Bexley Libraries and Museums Service
DES Graeme Campbell
exhibition

7 Japan
AD Tobu department store
AG Gallery Hashimoto
DIR/DES Ikko Tanaka
exhibition

50-51

1a-c

4

5

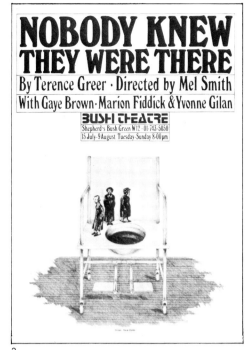

2

3

6

7

1a-c Germany
AD Hamburg Theatre
DES Holger Matthies
theatre

2 Great Britain
AD Bush Theatre
DES/ILL Oscar Zarate
theatre

3 Japan
AD Gallery Takega
AG Shigeo Okamoto Design Center
DIR/DES Shigeo Okamoto
ILL Toshiyuki Ohashi
exhibition

4 Japan
AD The Seibu Theater
DES Ikko Tanaka
ILL Haruo Takino
theatre

5 Great Britain
AD Oxford Playhouse
DES Bernard Canavan
theatre

6 Great Britain
AD Scottish Arts Council
AG James Gardiner Associates
DIR James Gardiner
DES Ian Woodyer
exhibition

7 United States
AD Student Services West
AG Gauger Sparks Silva
DIR/DES David Gauger
student travel, voyages d'étudiants,
Studentenreisen

1

2

3

5

6

SWISSAIR ▶ westafrica

4

Aerial photographs and panoramas: the village of Labbezanga

Photographs by George Gerster. Design Emil Schulthess

1 Great Britain
AD The Post Office
AG Philip Sharland Associates
DES Philip Sharland
stamp books, carnets de timbres-poste,
Briefmarkenheft

2 Great Britain
AD The Royal Society for the Prevention of
Accidents
DES Stan Krol
industrial safety, sécurité industrielle,
Unfallsverhütung

3 Hungary
AD Organizing Committee of 'Savaria Festival'
DIR/DES Nàndor Szilvàsy
opera

4 Switzerland
AD Swissair
DES Emil Schulthess
ILL George Gerster
tourism

5 Holland
AD Bureau CJP, Amersfoort
DES Gielijn Escher
youth festival, festival de jeunesse, Jugendfest

6 Hungary
AD Mokép
AG Magyar Hirdetö
DES Bakos István
film

Press advertisements
Annonces de presse
Zeitungs-Inserate

1a-g Italy
AD (a,d,e,f,g) Ing. C. Olivetti & C. S.p.A.
(b) British Olivetti Ltd
(c) Olivetti Corporation of America
AG Ufficio Pubblicita Olivetti S.P.P.
DIR (a,d,e,f,g) Giovanni Ferioli
(b) G. Ferioli, F. Ronchi
(c) G. Ferioli, I. Campagnoli
DES (a,d,e,f,g) Egidio Barborini
(b) Fulvio Ronchi
(c) Ines Campagnoli
ILL (a,f,g) Antionia Mulas
(b) Enzo Ragazzini
(c) Dudovich
COPY (a,d,e,f,g) Giovanni Guidici
(c) G. Giudici, G. Wintering
international promotion of office machines,
machines de bureau, Büro-machienen

d

e

1a

b

c

f

g

You'll find no hidden extras on a Thomson holiday.

1a–b–c

WHO GETS THE FIRST TASTE OF YOUR SPRING VEGETABLES?

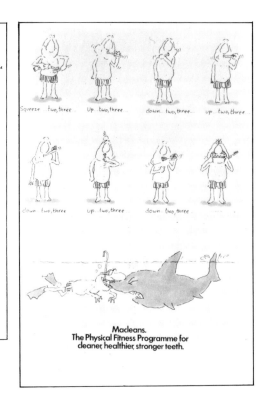

Macleans.
The Physical Fitness Programme for cleaner, healthier, stronger teeth.

3

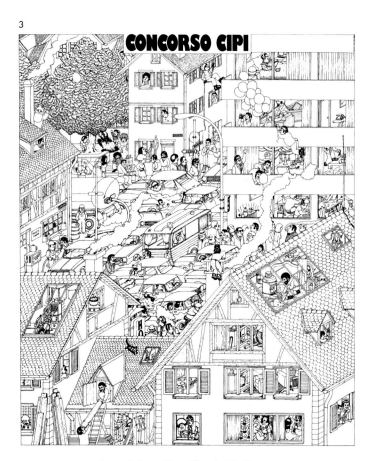

CONCORSO CIPI

Se non intervenite, qui brucia 33 volte tutto

4

Computers maken meer problemen dan zij kunnen oplossen.

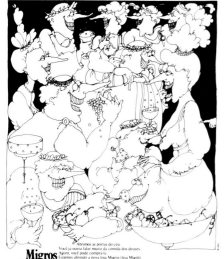

2a–b

5a–d

1a-c Great Britain
AD (a) Thomson Holidays
    (b) Jeyes (UK) Ltd
    (c) Beecham Group (Macleans)
AG Leo Burnett Ltd
DIR (a, c) Anthony Riggs
    (b) Chris Baker
ILL (b) Julian Graddon
    (c) Grey Jolliffe
COPY (a) Duncan Sinclair
    (b) Dan Levin
    (c) Bob Stanners
(a) packaged holidays
(b) antiseptic
(c) toothpaste, pâte dentifrice, Zahnpaste

2 a-b Brazil
AD Migros
AG Bureau Tecnico de Publicidade B.T.P. Ltda
DIR J. Natale Netto
DES Vicente C. Scorza
ILL Margherita Bornstein
COPY Walter Arruda
groceries, épicerie, Lebensmittel

3 Switzerland
AD Beratungsstelle für Brandverhütung Bern
AG Advico-Delpire
DIR Ruedi Külling
DES Röbi Hösli, Max Weber
ILL Alain Le Saux, Paris
fire prevention, service d'incendie,
Brandverhütung

4 Holland
AD IBM Nederland
AG Prad B.V.
DIR Wim Schols
COPY Dick Vos
computers

5a-d Spain
AD Laboratorios Rocador, S.A.
AG Pharma-Consult, S.A.
DIR Vicente Olmos
DES (a-c) Vicente Olmos
    (d) Javier Noguera
ILL (a-c) Joan Enric, Vicente Olmos
    (d) Joan Enric, Javier Noguera
pharmaceuticals

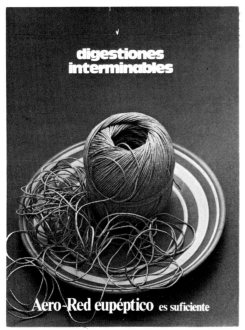

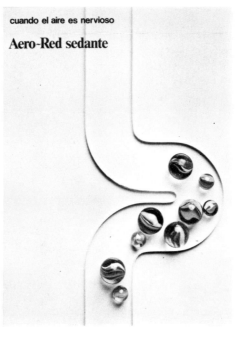

1

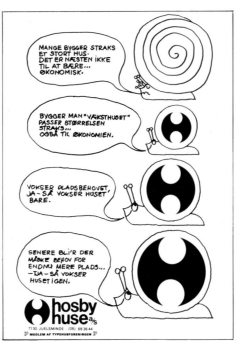

2

3

6a

(Gedicht von Algernon Charles Swinburne 1837–1909. Mode von Einhorn 1975.) David Hamilton fotografierte für Einhorn D 7402 Kirchentellinsfurt

6b

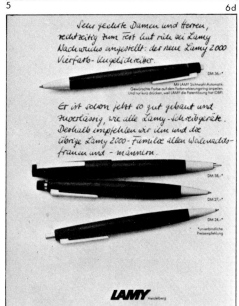

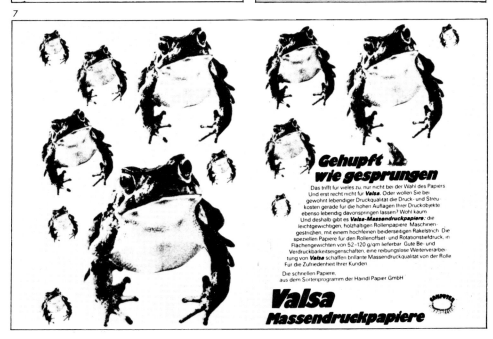

Press advertisements
Annonces de Presse
Zeitungs-Inserate

1 South Africa
AD Hayne and Gibson (Transvaal) Ltd
AG Derek Spaull Graphics
DIR/DES Derek Spaull
COPY Jean du Plessis
packaging, emballages, Verpackung

2 Denmark
AD Hosby Huse A/S.
AG weber & sørensen reklamebureau a/s
DIR/DES Ron Canham
COPY Erik Ansvang
prefabricated houses, maisons préfabriquécs,
Fertighaüser

3 India
AD Federal Republic of Germany New Delhi
AG Alfred Allan Advertising
DIR/DES Allan Luther
COPY J. Freise

4 United States
AD/AG Smith Kline & French Laboratories
DIR Alan Klawans
DES M. Hawley, A. Klawans
ILL Folon, France
COPY William Johnson
pharmaceuticals

5 Germany
AD Franz Westrich
AG Marex
DES Barbara Buchwald
stockings, bas, Hosen

6 Germany
AD (a,b,) Einhorn, Zeeb & Hornung
(c) IBM Deutschland GmbH
(d) Lamy GmbH
AG Leonhardt & Kern
DIR/DES (a) Uli Weber
(b) Peter Bamper
(c,d) Peter Vogt
ILL (a) David Hamilton, Paris
(b) Rolf Buder, Zürich
(c) Peter Vogt
(d) Jürgen Tapprich, Zürich
COPY (b) Uwe Mieske
(c,d) Hans Heger
(a,b) textiles
(c) computers
(d) writing materials, matériel d'écriture,
Schreibgeräte

7 Germany
AD Haindl Papier GmbH
AG Werbeberatung Peter Seidler
DIR Andreas Asam
DES Wolf Noack
ILL Bernhard Höhne
COPY Andreas Asam
paper

Wir haben die Natur kopiert:
«Naturform nahtlos».

Wir wollen, dass sich Frauen sicher fühlen.

Triumph
INTERNATIONAL

1975 beglückte der Inhalt dieser Dose Millionen von Frauen.

Was aus dieser Dose für den Busen kam,
kommt aus dieser Dose für den Po.

„Einer für alle" ist der durchschlagende Erfolg einer neuen, jungen Mieder-Generation, ein revolutionäres Produkt, das heute aus dem Miedermarkt nicht mehr wegzudenken ist. *Was dem BH diesen Erfolg brachte, wird den Erfolg dieses Höschens einleiten: Der „Einer für alle" WäscheSlip. Der WäscheSlip, der formt und paßt bis Größe 42. „Einer für alle", der WäscheSlip der neuen Mieder-Generation.* Mehr darüber von Ihrem Triumph-Berater.

Jünger
wird man nicht, aber…

kontaktfreudiger   aufgeschlossener

merkfähiger   lebensfroher

Encephabol

MERCK

1   2   3

6

Can Long Tall Sally find true happiness with a Fiat 127?

7a – b – c

If King George himself had appeared in driving cap and goggles, he could not have created more of a sensation than the one that occurred at the 1922 London Motor Show.

The cause of all the excitement is a new motor car that bears no frame, and no rigid front axle.

Motor engineers and enthusiasts alike are calling it a masterpiece and a tour de force.

It would be more correct however, to call it the Lancia Lambda.

It doesn't take an automotive engineer to realise that the Lambda is a very different automobile.

Gone is the squat, squared-off look we've become accustomed to, and to replace it, a slimmer, sleeker body.

The vehicle has been built on a "unitary construction" principle similar to the technique used in ships' hulls.

This has greatly reduced the weight of the car and greatly embarrassed the self-styled experts who have wondered just how the frame has been concealed.

The rigid front axle has been replaced by a suspension in which the wheels move independently of each other.

Finally, ample power and acceleration has been provided by a high-revving narrow V4 engine of 2120cc (130 cu. in.).

The Lancia Lambda has astounded experts, and shocked engineers.

It will delight drivers.

Introducing the 1922 Lancia.

The previous Lancia, the D20, boasted the first ever six cylinder engine designed exclusively for competition.

This made it an extremely hard car for the Lancia company to follow.

It was driven in major competitions like the Monza Grand Prix, Targa Florio and Catania-Etna by drivers like Bonetto, Maglioli, Biondetti and Castellotti.

This made it an extremely hard car for other drivers to overtake.

Nevertheless, the Lancia company was convinced it could do better.

What it did was produce the D24.

The engine has been stretched to 3284 cc with a bore and stroke of 88 x 90.

The power output has been boosted to 265 hp at 6500 rpm. The top speed has been accelerated to 265 kph.

And the handling has been enhanced by shortening the wheelbase, repositioning the gear box to place more weight over the rear axle and replacing the transverse leaf spring rear suspension with two longitudinal semi springs fixed to the chassis in the front.

If this technical information is a little difficult to understand in print, it will become devastatingly clear on the track.

Earlier in the year, four Lancia D24s were entered in the Panamerican Carrera event, and between them won no less than six of the eight stages.

Outright victory went to Lancia driver Juan Fangio, who may yet become as legendary as the D24 itself.

Introducing the 1953 Lancia.

In the likely event that you never had a chance to get your hands on a 1925 Lambda, that somehow the 1931 Dilambda escaped your clutches and that you missed out once again on the 1933 Astura, we'd like to bring the 1975 Beta Coupe to your attention while

you can still buy one without having to break the bank.

Of course, for many reasons, we can't guarantee that in twenty years the 1975 Lancia Beta Coupe won't also be a beautiful car at a ridiculous price.

The first of these reasons is a transverse 1.8 litre overhead cam engine.

Another is the reinforced safety cage which surrounds the passenger compartment and makes it likely the car will survive long enough to become a classic.

Nevertheless, the Beta Coupe is more than just a good investment.

It's also a 2+2 that not only handles like an expensive well bred Italian sports coupe, but also looks like one.

At a casual glance, the Beta Coupe looks convincingly able to take on the worst conditions. At a closer examination, it's not hard to see why.

Front wheel drive, independent suspension, rack and pinion steering and disc brakes and radials all round make the 1975 Lancia Beta Coupe a rare car indeed.

For this reason, we suggest you see your Lancia dealer soon, whether you want it for yourself, your wife or your collection.

Introducing the 1975 Lancia Coupe.

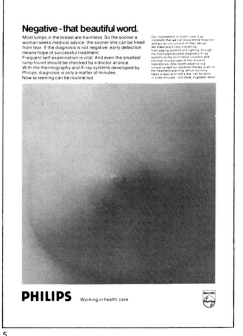

1 Germany
AD Triumph Universal
AG Adolf Wirz AG
DIR/DES F. Bader
bras, soutien-gorge, Büstenhalter

2 Germany
AD Triumph International
AG Apollon
DIR/DES Lutz Roeder
women's underwear, lingerie, Unterwäsche

3 Switzerland
AD E. Merck
AG Institut Dr. Friesewinkel
DES Maya Stange
pharmaceuticals

4 Sweden
AD RFSU
AG Faltman & Malmen AB
DIR Gunnar Faltman
DES Lars Zakrisson
ILL Atelje Sterneck
family planning, familles plannés,
Geburtskontrolle

5 Holland
AD N.V. Philips' Gloeilampenfabrieken
AG Nationale Publiciteits Onderneming BV
DIR/DES Theo Stradman
COPY Derek Beck
lamps

6 Australia
AD Fiat of Australia Pty Ltd
G Grey Advertising Pty Ltd
DIR/DES Tony Stewart
motor-cars, autos

7a-c Australia
AD Fiat of Australia Pty Ltd
AG Grey Advertising Pty Ltd
DIR/DES Bart Pavlovich
ILL John Street
motor-cars, autos

8 Great Britain
AD/AG Tutssel/Warne
DIR/DES Glenn Tutssel
carpentry and joinery, menuiserie, Tischlerei

9 Italy
AD Circle-Radio Commercial
AG House Agency
DIR Carlo Cavallini
COPY Bruno Esposito
radio commercials

10 Spain
AD Guillamet
AG SCACS
DIR Federico Anguera
DES Salvatore Adduci
COPY Ricardo Castrillejo
statistics

Press advertisements
Annonces de Presse
Zeitungs-Inserate

1a-c Holland
AD (a-b) Het Nederlands Zuivelbureau
(c) Seven-Up Nederland
AG Prad B.V.
DIR (a) Peter Boezewinkel
(b) Joop Smit, Karel Meijers
(c) Joop Smit
ILL (a) Keith McEwan
(b) Karel Meijers
(c) Nicolas Price
COPY (a-b) Paul Mertz
(c) Jolle Westermann
(a-b) milk, lait
(c) non-alcoholic drinks

2a-b Germany
AD Ihring-Melchior, Lich
AG SSM-Schlüter Schürmann Mehl
DIR Harald Schlüter/Jürgen Mehl
beer, bière, Bier

3 Great Britain
AD Whitbread & Co
AG Collett, Dickenson, Pearce & Ptners Ltd
DIR/DES Alan Waldi
ILL Michael Terry
beer, bière, Bier

4 Germany
AD Swiss Cheese Union Inc.
AG DFS & R Dorland Werbeagentur
DIR/DES Hans Andersch
ILL H. R. Disch
COPY Gotz Wengler, D. Tomczak
cheese, fromage, Käse

5 Holland
AD NZB Dutch Dairy Corporation
AG NPO-Nationale Publiciteits Onderneming B.V.
DIR/DES Huib Ebbinge
ILL Diet van Beeck
COPY Joop Cranendonk
dairy products

1a–b–c

4

5

Natur frei Haus.

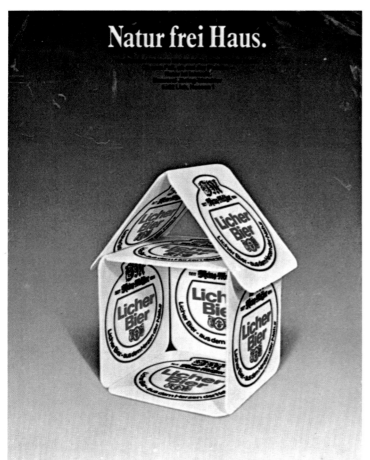

Licher Bier. Aus dem Herzen der Natur.

Evergreen seit 1854.

Licher Bier. Aus dem Herzen der Natur.

2a–b

3

Heineken. Refreshes the parts other beers cannot reach.

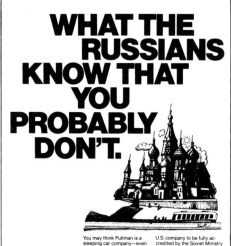

1a-c

2a-b

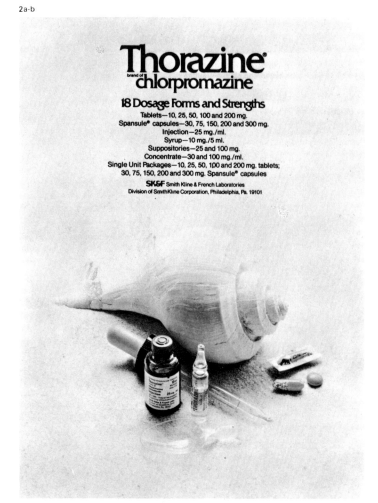

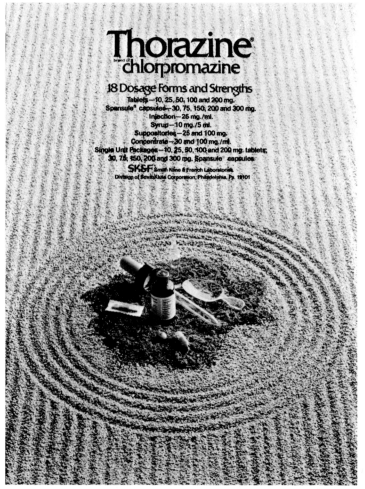

Our major competition.

This is still the primary distribution system in much of the world today.

Donkeys. Horses. Oxen. And even head-laden, back-strapped humans taking their food and products to market.

We aren't ignoring the companies who compete with us in producing freight cars, transit cars, truck trailers and containers.

(There's burgeoning growth in the U.S. and Canada alone. Transportation requirements are expected to increase from today's 2.7 billion level to 5.7-billion ton-miles by the year 2000.)

Yet, there's an even greater marketplace and greater potential beyond.

With a world population growth of 65% expected over the next few decades, our skills, products, and services are needed as never before.

By choice or circumstances, our work involves every major socio-industrial priority on the planet: energy, steel, food, environment, transportation. We strive to bring to each job not just technological leadership, but a kind of global

vision alert to basic human needs.

And a desire to outdo the competition wherever it exists.

Pullman incorporated

200 South Michigan Avenue, Chicago, Illinois 60604

1d

3

750 WEST PENDER & DOWNTOWN VANCOUVER

4

New Priorities/New Directions

Crude Alternatives

The oil shortage has driven home a vital if unpleasant message:

Unless we're willing to adjust to a lower standard of living we must begin to devise new ways to meet our growing energy needs.

The scene depicted here is admittedly quixotic. But these giant fiberglass windmills which might be made with our petrochemical materials (AMOCO Isophthalic Acid and Polypropylene) serve to make a point.

Oil can't be an unending fuel for heat and electricity. But we can refine some crude into petrochemicals to be used in products that conserve energy. And even bring new sources into everyday life.

For instance Amoco's petrochemicals have been employed in architectural insulation, carpeting, drapes and blankets. And might be used in reflectors and heatshields that can retain heat in winter, reduce heat gains in summer.

How can we beat the energy shortage? Perhaps the windmill won't. But the mind will.

So even though there are some current material shortages, Amoco is pursuing developmental activity with customers against the time when supplies are not as restricted.

As you are working on new answers, think of us.

Amoco Chemicals Department 12230A MC4102 200 E. Randolph Drive Chicago Illinois 60601

Amoco Chemicals Corporation

1a-d United States
AD Pullman Inc.
AG BBDM Inc.
DIR/DES (a,b) John Dolby,
(c,d) Gary Melzer
ILL (a,b) Bill Vulksonivich
(d) John Dolby
trains

2a-b United States
AD/AG Smith Kline & French Laboratories
DIR J. Robert Parker
DES Ford-Byrne
ILL Leonard Cohen
COPY Norm Flagg
pharmaceuticals

3 Canada
AD Hammerson Property Corp. Ltd
AG Raymond Lee & Assoc. Ltd
DIR/DES Raymond Lee
ILL Ron Hills
COPY Barbara Boydon
property

4 United States
AD Amoco Chemicals Corp.
AG BBDM Inc.
DIR/DES John Dolby, Gary Melzer
ILL Howard Levant
oil shortage, crise de pétrole, Petroleumcrise

1

2a

2b

2c

2d

3

"O pai da minha primeira namorada tinha um Chevrolet."

General Motors
50 anos de Brasil

4

1 Denmark
AD Association of curtain dealers
AG Benton & Bowles
DIR John Andersen
COPY Ole Drogh
curtains, rideaux, Vorhänge

2a-d Italy
AD (a,b) Perlier S.p.A.,
    (c) Comitato Moda Casa
    (d) GBG Gambarotta
AG B Communications
DES B Communications Creative Group
(a,b) cosmetics, (c) table linen, linge de table,
Tischzeug, (d) brandy, cognac

3 Brazil
AD General Motors do Brasil
AG DPZ-Duailibi, Petit, Zaragoza Propaganda
S.A.
DIR Francisco Petit
ILL Moacyr Lugato
COPY Washington Olivetto
motor-cars, autos

4 United States
AD Victor Comptometer Corp.
AG BBDM
DIR/DES John Dolby
ILL Bus Gregory
calculators

Bovis: The builder with a cure for cardiac arrest.

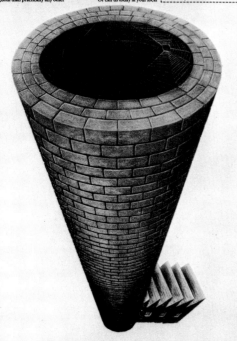

How to breed monsters.
(and how not to).

1a-b

3

Lourdeurs d'estomac qui montent à la tête.
maux de tête qui tombent sur l'estomac…

Alka-Seltzer

4

Avis.
Was für einen Wagen Sie auch brauchen.

Avis
Autovermietung

Michelangelo, Elisabetta & amici si sono messi in società.

2

5 6

A walk in San Francisco is a treat.

When the destination is David's, our city's celebrated deli/restaurant. Step out of the Fairmont's lobby and stroll West one block past Huntington Park to the corner of California and Taylor. Turn left and gently coast down Nob Hill's Taylor Street to Geary. Then a few steps to your left is where all the zesty treats of real home-style Jewish cookery await you.

For the journey back up Nob Hill, take any Cable Car at Union Square (two blocks East). We'll pack you a goodie to sweeten the ride.

Geary near Taylor
771-1600

DAVID'S
Deli/Restaurant
We're open when you need us.

Preview the Villas [de San] Alma. Walk through a little sawd[ust]. Be one of the first to see the 26 l[uxuriou]e cluster homes under construction in Palo Alto. The Villas de San Alma are designed with 3 bedrooms, gourmet kitchens, breakfast rooms, hide-away lofts, interior courtyards and more. Come see for yourself today.

Villas de San Alma

Villas de San Alma · Mayfield Mall
Alma St · Central Expwy
Palo Alto

For more information call 494-2155 or 961-1441. Homes from $62,950 to $75,950.
A project of Dividend Industries Inc.

7

Many persons who are unable to attend dance events at regular prices are eligible to purchase TDF's Dance Voucher. Students, teachers, union members, retired persons, performing arts professionals, among others, can qualify.

A set of five vouchers costs only $5.00 and may be used as admission at hundreds of dance events in New York City. Voucher holders receive the New York Dance Calendar monthly. To order vouchers, please write to Theatre Development Fund, 1564 Broadway, New York City, 10036 requesting mailing list application and dance voucher order forms.

1a-b Great Britain
AD Bovis Construction
AG Peter Maisey Co. Ltd
DES Peter Maisey
construction company

2 Italy
AD EEC (European Economic Community)
AG Promos
DIR/DES Bob Elliott, Brian Murrels
ILL Wurlitzer Studios, London
COPY Pia de Fazio
children's magazine, periodique d'enfants, Kinderzeitschrift

3 Belgium
AD Laboratoires Miles
AG Dechy Univas
DIR Dan Miletic
DES Christian Marchal
COPY Roger Habran
pharmaceutical

4 Switzerland
AD Avis
AG Adolf Wirz AG
DIR/DES M. Willuweit
COPY R. Biedermann
car rental service

5 United States
AD David's Deli, Restaurant
AG Gauger Sparks Silva
DIR/DES David Gauger
restaurant

6 United States
AD Dividend Industries, Inc.
AG Gauger Sparks Silva
DIR/DES Walter Sparks
COPY Larry Silva
housing development scheme, plan de construction immobiliére, Siedlungsplan

7 United States
AD Theatre Development Fund
AG Charles Fuhrman Edith Allgood Graphic Design
DIR/DES Charles Fuhrman
ILL Edith Allgood
ticket vouchers for dance programme, bon pour programme de danse, Billet für Tanzprogram

1

2

3

5

Three Towns lättöl.
Lite mildare. Lite rundare. Lite alkohol.
Den rätta drycken till en nyfiskad, grillad abborre.

THE PUMP AND THE FIZZ

Jack and Bill just had a thrill
When they fetched the water.
Fizz they found and drank two rounds,
And soon burst out in laughter.
Up Jack got and asked what's what,
And why the fizzy caper,
Fizz is wizz, for bottler's bizz,
When pumped by Ajax, the master.

With capacities to 2500 G.P.M., heads to 300 feet. Ajax pumps are designed to service filtration processes and other applications as required by soft drink manufacturers of Australia.

Ajax single stage centrifugal pumps sizes 1¼" to 8" are made in stainless steel, bronze, iron, S.G. iron, ni-resist, G75A, Hastalloy and others.

Manufacturers and suppliers of industrial, commercial, agricultural and domestic pumps.

McPHERSON'S LIMITED
Pump Division
Melbourne 62 0301,
Sydney 51 0433, Brisbane 5 0191
Adelaide 46 0271, Perth 6 3211.

THE PUMP AND THE BOOZE

Mash out the barrel,
We'll have a barrel of wort,
Mash out the barrel,
We'll have a jolly good snort.
Wort out the barrel,
We'll have a barrel of fun,
Wort out the barrel,
Ajax gets beer on the run.

With capacities to 2500 G.P.M., heads to 300 feet. Ajax pumps are used on mash tubs, sparging tanks and other applications as required by breweries, distillers and winemakers.

Ajax single stage centrifugal pumps sizes 1¼" to 8" are made in stainless steel, bronze, iron, S.G. iron, ni-resist, G75A, Hastalloy and others.

Manufacturers and suppliers of industrial, commercial, agricultural and domestic pumps.

McPHERSON'S LIMITED
Pump Division
Melbourne 62 0301,
Sydney 51 0433, Brisbane 5 0191
Adelaide 46 0271, Perth 6 3211.

4a–b

6a–d

1 Great Britain
AD Cadbury Bros Ltd
AG Leo Burnett Ltd
DIR/DES Stewart Howard
ILL John Thornton
COPY David O'Connor Thomson
chocolate

2 Switzerland
AD Schweiz. Obstverband, Zug
AG Gisler & Gisler
DIR/DES Erich Harmann
ILL Ernst Wirz
COPY Peter Schulz
applejuice, jus de pomme, Apfelsaft

3 Australia
AD Stafford-Miller Ltd
AG Grey Advertising Pty Ltd
DIR/DES Tony Stewart
ILL John Ashenhurst
denture adhesive, fixatif pour dentiers,
Gebissfixativ

4a-b Australia
AD McPhersons Ltd
AG E. G. Holt & Associates
DIR George Conte, Janet Carr
DES Janet Carr
COPY Murray Ukena
pumps

5 Sweden
AD AB Pripps Bryggerier
AG Fältman & Malmen AB
DIR Gunnar Fältman
DES Lars Zakrisson
ILL Carl-Johan Rönn
beer, bière, Bier

6a-d Denmark
AD Daoplast AS
AG Mogens Raffel
DIR/DES Johnny Lund
ILL Finn Andersen
sewer pipes, canalisation

1

2

3

5a-b

Ontem à noite,
Serginho participou de um assassinato,
viu uma mulher fugir com o amante e
aprendeu como se assalta um banco.

Adivinha o que ele vai ser quando crescer?

A mãe do Serginho sempre achou que ele era um garoto problema.

Imagine que ele nem bem deixou de engatinhar e já começou a chutar bola na sala, melecar as paredes com as mãos sujas de doce, estragar roupinhas novas num instante, pintar o sete.

Depois, veio a época da escola e a coisa ficou pior ainda: era um tal de amiguinho todo dia dentro de casa, uma barulheira insuportável, aquelas crianças correndo, um inferno.

Até que um dia a mãe de Serginho descobriu que havia um jeito de fazer com que ele ficasse quieto, sozinho e bem comportado durante horas e horas. Era só ligar a televisão.

Batata.

Desde esse dia tudo mudou: agora Serginho chega da escola, almoça, faz a lição correndo, senta na frente da televisão e só desliga na hora de ir pra cama.

E a mãe dele vive sossegada.

Só que ela não devia viver tão sossegada, não.

Porque Serginho tem assistido na televisão uma série de programas que ele não devia assistir. E aprendido uma série de coisas que ele não devia aprender.

Ontem mesmo ele viu um filme que deixou muito adulto impressionado. Mas ele nem-te-ligo. Até vibrou com aquela estória da mulher bolar o assassinato do marido, fugir com aquele cara de barba e depois assaltar o banco.

Você acha que ele é um caso perdido?

Nós não. Nós achamos que o caso perdido é a mãe dele.

Porque, quando uma mulher transforma um aparelho de TV na babá eletrônica de seu filho, ela está jogando com o futuro dessa criança. E roubando dela a parte mais bonita e gostosa da vida: a infância.

Nós da Colorado estamos tocando nesse assunto porque nós fabricamos televisores há muito tempo.

Sempre preocupados em fazer um aparelho que mereça a confiança dos senhores pais.

Ainda agora nós fizemos um acordo com a Blaupunkt para produzir no Brasil tudo que existir de mais ousado no mundo dos televisores.

E já começamos lançando um TV digital a cores que muda de canal assim que você encosta o dedo no seletor.

Acontece que tudo isso pode ser ótimo para a sua comodidade, mas não tem a mínima importância diante do futuro do seu filho.

Por isso, nós resolvemos fazer este apelo a você e a todas as mães. Principalmente as comodistas.

Procure selecionar os programas de TV que o seu filho assiste da mesma maneira que você seleciona a escola que ele freqüenta, as roupas que ele veste ou as companhias com que ele anda.

Nem que pra isso seja preciso sacrificar alguns programas que você gosta e são próprios para a sua idade, ou agüentar as traquinagens que são normais numa criança.

Não esqueça que, mesmo com uma criação cuidadosa, hoje em dia anda muito difícil prever o que uma criança vai ser quando crescer.

Já pensou então se você deixar essa criança abandonada aos perigos de uma televisão?

COLORADO
Agora com tecnologia Blaupunkt.

4

6

Happy New Year.

Compared to this recession, few economic downturns have been so widely heralded, with such cordial acceptance by the experts.

Still, in the face of it all, we think the times are ripe for improving your business, just as we've been improving ours.

Not necessarily with "business as usual." (When has business ever been "usual?")

But by preparing for change, being alert to it, responsive to it, and acting accordingly.

Sure. A lot of companies are going to lose money.

But some companies will make more than ever.

Some will panic, stumble, retrench, and shrink. Others will toughen and expand.

We believe that the smart businessman must accept changing economic climates as readily as he accepts the changing seasons.

And we have prepared a booklet that can help you deal with the changes ahead.

It's called: "Marketing for Profit in a Business Recession."

We are not, obviously, presuming to solve your problems with a single brochure.

But we are offering to share some workable strategy that can help you live through 1975 more comfortably.

If you're in marketing or management, you should have a copy. And a smile on your face.

Simply attach the coupon to your letterhead.

To:
W. S. Browning
BBDM, Inc.
233 E. Ontario St.
Chicago, Illinois 60611

Yes, please send me, free and without obligation, a copy of your new brochure entitled, "Marketing for Profit in a Business Recession."

Name _____
Title _____
Company _____
Address _____
City _____ State _____ Zip _____

BBDM

BBDM Advertising, 233 E. Ontario St., Chicago, Illinois 60611 (312) 943-5445

We serve the following companies: Victor Comptometer · Sherwood Electronics · Holiday Inn (Milwaukee and Indiana Districts) · Henry M. Goodman Furniture Stores · Cleveland/Jackson Furniture Mfg · Franklin Picture Frames · Hawthorn Mellody Dairy · Mellody Lane Foods · International Harvester Trucks (Projects) · Open Court Publishing · Amoco Chemicals Corporation · Stetson Discount Stores · Elgin Watch

2

1

5

6

3

4 a–b

**Press advertisements
Annonces de Presse
Zeitungs-Inserate**

1 Great Britain
AD Chivers
AG Ted Bates Ltd
DIR Alan Lofts
marmalade

2 Great Britain
AD/AG Josiah Wedgwood & Sons Ltd
DES Zaccarini/Barrevoets, Milan
porcelain

3 Greece
AD Seventeen Cosmetics
AG K&K Univas Advertising Centre
DIR F. V. Carabott
DES Agni Katzourakis
ILL Mavroyenis
COPY Pavlina Pambouthi
cosmetics

4a-b Germany
AD Gainsborough Cosmetics
AG Herter, Urban & Co
DIR/DES Dieter Urban
COPY Rudolf O. Herter
cosmetics

5 Israel
AD Belmon Ltd
AG O.K. Advertising Ltd
DIR/DES Abe Rosenfeld
ILL Yona Flink
cosmetics

6 Israel
AD Gibor
AG Zvi Karmon Advertising
DIR/DES Yak Molho
ILL Ben Lamm
COPY Yehoshua Ron
panty hose

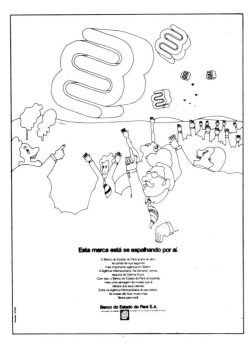

Esta marca está se espalhando por aí.

O Banco do Estado do Pará acaba de abrir
as portas de sua segunda
mais importante agência em Belém.
A Agência Metropolitana. Na Senador Lemos,
esquina de Duthra Dutra.
Com isso, o Banco do Estado do Pará acrescenta
mais uma vantagem às muitas que já
oferece aos seus clientes.
Entre na Agência Metropolitana do seu banco.
As coisas vão ficar muito mais
fáceis para você.

Banco do Estado do Pará S.A.

Because two heads can be better than one.

It wasn't what you'd call a long flight. One-hundred and twenty feet to be exact. Air time: 12 seconds. But until Orville and Wilbur Wright put their heads together to really study the problems of flight, it seemed that mankind's oldest dream would never become a reality. Yet it did, on that famous day in December, 1903, and the fascinating era of aviation was on its way.

That remarkable feat by the Wright brothers is just one example of what can happen when people work together toward a common goal. And that's pretty much the idea behind Montana Banks: fourteen banks throughout the state who've joined forces to share ideas about better ways to serve their customers.

For example, we'll be exploring new services and new methods to keep us operating at top efficiency. And though we think sharing ideas is an improved way of doing business, we also want you to know that it won't replace any bank's individuality. Keep in mind that we're still the same people with the same goal of providing you with quality service tailored to meet your specific needs. But as the story of the Wright brothers shows, two heads can be better than one.

Montana Banks
First National Montana Bank of Missoula
   formerly The First National Bank
Montana Bank of Absarokee, N.A.
Montana Bank of Baker, N.A.
Montana Bank of Belgrade
Montana Bank of Bozeman, N.A.
Montana Bank of Browning, N.A.
Montana Bank of Butte, N.A.
Montana Bank of Circle, N.A.
Montana Bank of Fairview
Montana Bank of Mineral County
Montana Bank of South Missoula
   formerly First State Bank
Montana Bank of Red Lodge, N.A.
Montana Bank of Richey, N.A.
Montana Bank of Roundup, N.A.

Montana Banks

2

Wir sind immer schon mit der Zeit gegangen

Wie oft sich der Geschmack für Heim- und Raumkultur seither auch geändert hat: wir waren immer maßgeblich daran beteiligt, für das jeweilige WOHNBEHAGEN zu sorgen.

Litega

ÖSTERREICHS GRÖSSTER RAUMAUSSTATTER
mit der traditionellen Fachberatung in 32 Filialen

Bodenbeläge · Teppichboden · Teppiche · Vorhänge

Wien 1 · Kärntnerstraße 1	Wien 16 · Ottakringer Straße 39
Wien 1 · Kärntnerstraße 63	Wien 17 · Kalvarienberggasse 46
Wien 1 · Wollzeile 13	Wien 20 · Wallensteinstraße 16
Wien 2 · Taborstraße 29	Wien 21 · Am Spitz 2-3
Wien 3 · Landstr. Hauptstraße 32	Wien 22 · Wagramer Straße 139
Wien 5 · Schönbrunner Straße 105	Linz · Landstraße 38
Wien 6 · Mariahilfer Straße 35	Linz · Wiener Straße 41
Wien 8 · Mariahilfer Straße 104	Salzburg · Platzl 2
Wien 8 · Lerchenfelder Straße 164	Innsbruck · Anichstraße 3
Wien 9 · Alser Straße 20	Feldkirch · Montfortgasse 15
Wien 9 · Alserbachstraße 12	Klagenfurt · Villacher Straße 1
Wien 10 · Favoritenstraße 97	Graz · Murgasse 3
Wien 10 · Hansson-Zentrum	Wiener Neustadt
Favoritenstraße 238	Herzog Leopold-Straße 30
Wien 11 · Simmeringer Hauptstraße 111	Schwechat · Wiener Straße 10
Wien 13 · Hietzinger Hauptstraße 22	St. Pölten · Bahnhofplatz 12
Wien 15 · Mariahilfer Straße 191	Bruck/Mur · Herzog Ernst Gasse 28

3

6

Klerkegades største reklamebureau bli'r nu verdens niende største.

I går Danmark, i dag EF, i morgen? Som et godt bureau har vi et ansvar. Også i fremtiden. Vi må vide, hvad der rør sig på det internationale marked. Ikke blot på overfladen, men indefra. Og det erfarer bedst på én måde. Ved selv at være international. Derfor hedder hedder Weber & Sørensen, København Benton & Bowles A/S, fra den 1. december. Det er sket ved, at Weber & Sørensen, Århus har overdraget sin aktieandel til Benton & Bowles Inc., New York. For god ordens skyld skal nævnes, at denne overdragelse ikke berører Weber & Sørensen, Århus' fremtidige virke.

W&S København har lige siden starten, for 10 år siden, gennemlevet en forrygende udvikling. I dag er vi et godt kreativt bureau, med sund økonomi, og en solid kundekreds. Og hvorfor så Benton & Bowles. Benton & Bowles har væsentlige fortrin.

For det første er det en af verdens bedste og største bureau-kæder. Med en omsætning alene i U.S.A. på 200 mill. $. For det andet, er Benton & Bowles' policy, at alle dets internationale bureauer er selvstændigt arbejdende og ledet. Og for det tredie, vi har kendt og samarbejdet med Benton & Bowles i mere end 2 år. Det har været særdeles inspirerende.

Derfor fortsætter vi samarbejdet. Nu blot forstærket. John Andersen og Henning Harboe fortsætter som ledere og aktie-medindehavere af bureauet. Adressen, Klerkegade 19 og tlf. (01) 14 32 11 er uændret.

For vore kunder betyder det ikke blot et andet navn. På længere sigt betyder det, at vi kan tilbyde international kontakt. Og endnu bedre international markedsviden. Ikke mindst på det skandinaviske område.

Vil De lære os nærmere at kende. Og få en mere grundig præsentation af Benton & Bowles, så ring til os.

Vi arbejder i dag med:
Belgisk Import Co. A/S: Bolex filmudstyr - Co-Ro Food A/S: Sunquick frugtkoncentrater - D.E.R. A/S: Udlejning af TV - The International Meehanite: Støbegods - Junckers Savværk A/S: Parketgulve, Blitsa - Nestle Nordisk Akta.: Maggi, Storkøkken Service, Automat Service - Chr. Rasmussen A/S: Møbler - A.H. Riise: Sea & Ski og Indoor/Outdoor - A.V. Rørsgaard & Co. A/S: Max Factor kosmetik - Mr. Smith's Hobbyland: Fritids- og havecenter - Thorn Lampe A/S · Thorn Kenwood A/S - Thorn Radio A/S · Suhrtral A/S - Hafnia-Haand I Haand A/S · Höganäs A/S: Bygningskeramik og Cuprinol.

W&S svarer Benton & Bowles fra 1. dec.

7

- Det bästa med bastun är en kall öl efteråt.

- Det känner jag varmt för.

Three Towns II B
Lite mildare. Lite rundare. Lite godare.

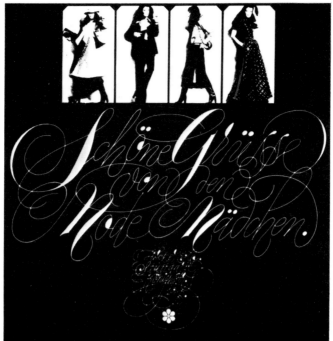

Press advertisements
Annonces de Presse
Zeitungs-Inserate

1 Brazil
AD Banco do Estado do Pará S.A.
AG Mendes Publicidade Ltda
DIR/DES Osmar Pinheiro Jr
bank

2 United States
AD Montana Banks
AG Bonnie Dean Marketing
DIR/DES Bob Coonts
COPY Carol Kanouff
group of banks

3 Austria
AD Litega AU.
AG Graphik Studio Hauch
DIR/DES Walter J. Hauch

4 Switzerland
AD Reisebüro Kuoni AG
AG Adolf Wirz AG
DIR T. Scherrer
DES W. Bühler
COPY F. Hunziker
travel, voyage, Reisen

5 Germany
AD Tischer & Co.
AG/DES Peter Steiner
DIR C. A. Froh
ILL Studio Heinrich
COPY C. A. Froh
fashion, Mode

6 Denmark
AD/AG Benton & Bowles
DIR John Andersen
ILL Finn Rosted
COPY Ole Krogh
self-promotion

7 Sweden
AD AB Pripps Bryggerier
AG Fältman & Malmen AB
DIR Gunnar Fältman
DES Claes Henning
ILL Atelje Sterneck
beer

8 Brazil
AD Metais Sanitários Deca
AG DPZ-Duailibi, Petit, Zaragoza
DIR José Zaragoza
ILL Moacyr Lugato
COPY João Augusto Palhares Neto
sanitary appliances

9 Brazil
AD Rações Abhanguera
AG DPZ-Duailibi, Petit, Zaragoza
DIR Hector Tortolano
DES Delcio & Flavio
COPY Laurence Klinger
poultry food, aliments pour volaille,
Geflügelfutter

Typefaces

Caractères

Schrifttypen

Bookjackets

Chemises de Livres

Buchumschläge

1 Norway
AD Norsk Bokklubben
DES Hansjørgen Toming
bookcovers, bindings for bookclub, reliure de
livres, Buchbindung

2 Great Britain
AD Mushroom Studio
AG Hat Studio
DIR/DES David Wakefield
ILL Alan Cracknell
COPY Terry Comer
phototypesetting

1.

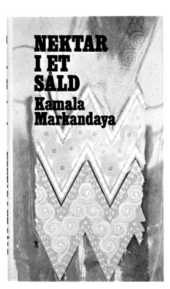

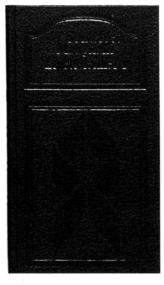
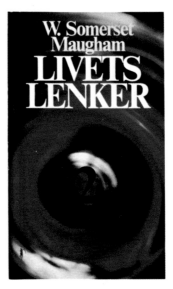

Mushroom's Alphabets.

100 St Martin's Lane, London WC2N 4AZ. Telephone 01-637 0068.

These are the typefaces we can supply you with any day of the week. And many of them are exclusive to us. But even more exclusive are those we can't supply on demand. Let's explain.
If you want a new typeface designed, or an old one for use on the typositor, we can make a film font in about three days.
From then on it's exclusively yours for six months or for as long as the campaign featuring it lasts.
So if you can't find the face you want here just ask for it and it's yours.

Abbey *
Abbey Bold *
Advertisers Gothic Light
Advertisers Gothic
Advertisers Gothic Condensed
Antique Olive
Antique Olive Italic
Antique Olive Narrow
Antique Olive Medium
Antique Olive Bold
Antique Olive Nord
Arnholm Sans Medium
Avant Garde Gothic Extra Light
Avant Garde Gothic Book
Avant Garde Gothic Medium
Avant Garde Gothic Demi
Avant Garde Gothic Bold

Basilea
Baskerville 169 *
Baskerville 169 Italic *
Baskerville Old Face
Baskerville Old Face Italic
Baskerville Bold 312 *
BASKERVILLE BOLD CONDENSED TITLING *
Bauer Classic Roman
Bauer Bodoni
Bauer Bodoni Italic
Bodoni Book
Bodoni Bold
Bembo
Bembo Italic
Bembo Bold
Beton Bold
Beton Bold Condensed
Beton Extra Bold
Bookman
Bookman Italic and Swashes
Bookman Bold and Swashes *
Bookman Bold Outline and Swashes
BROADWAY
Broadway Bold

BUSORAMA MEDIUM
BUSORAMA BOLD

* Candida
* Candida Italic
* Candida Medium
Caslon 471
Caslon 471 Italic and Swashes
Caslon 540
Caslon 540 Italic
Caslon 641
Caslon Bold
Caslon Adbold
Caslon Old Face Heavy
Caslon Antique
Caslon Antique Italic
Century Schoolbook
Century Schoolbook Italic
Century Schoolbook Bold
Century Bold
Century Old Style
Century Old Style Bold
Century Expanded
Century Nova
Century Nova Italic
Centaur
Centaur Italic
Cheltenham Old Style
Cheltenham Old Style Condensed
Cheltenham Medium
Cheltenham Medium Italic

Cheltenham Bold
Cheltenham Bold Italic
Cheltenham Bold Condensed
Cheltenham Bold Extended
Clearface Bold
Clearface Heavy
Clearface Heavy Condensed
Clearface Gothic Bold
Clearface Gothic Extra Bold
Cloister Old Style
Cloister Bold
Cloister Bold Italic and Swashes
Cochin Old Style N°61
Colwell Handletter
Concorde *
Concorde Semi-Bold *
Consort
Cooper Old Style
Cooper Black
Cooper Black Italic

Garamond Old Style
Garamond Old Style Italic
Garamond Old Style Bold Italic
Garamond Old Style Extra Bold
Gill Sans Light
Gill Sans Light Italic
Gill Sans Medium
Gill Sans Medium Italic
Gill Sans Bold
Gill Sans Bold Condensed
Gill Sans Bold Extra Condensed
GILL SANS BOLD TITLING
Gill Sans Extra Bold
* GILL SANS EXTRA BOLD CONDENSED TITLING 373
Gill Sans Ultra Bold
* GILL SANS CAMEO 233
Goudy Old Style
Goudy Old Style Italic

Goudy Catalogue
Goudy Bold
Goudy Extra Bold
Goudy Heavyface
Goudy Heavyface Condensed
Granby Light *
Granby Medium
Granby Bold
Granby Extra Bold
Granby Elephant
Grotesque N°9
Grotesque N°215 *
Grotesque N°216 *

Deepdene
Domino
Domning Antiqua
Doni
* Don't Script
* Dulip

EAGLE BOLD
Eastern Souvenir Light
Eastern Souvenir Medium
Eastern Souvenir Bold
* Eastern Souvenir Extra Bold
ECLAIR
* Ehrhardt
* Ehrhardt Semi-Bold
* Ehrhardt Extra Bold (Williams)
* Ehrhardt Ultra Bold (Williams)

Harry Thin
Harry Plain
Harry Heavy
Harry Fat
Harry Obese
Helvetica Light
Helvetica Light Italic
Helvetica
Helvetica Italic
Helvetica Medium
Helvetica Medium Italic
Helvetica Bold
Horley Old Style
Horley Old Style Medium
Horley Old Style Bold
Horley Old Face Heavy 188

Fanfare
FAST LADY *
Franklin Gothic
Franklin Gothic Condensed
Franklin Gothic Condensed Italic
Franklin Gothic Extra Condensed
Franklin Gothic Wide
Friz Quadrata
Futura Light
Futura Light Oblique

Futura Book
Futura Medium
Futura Demi-Bold
Futura Bold
Futura Bold Condensed
Futura Extra Bold
Futura Extra Bold Condensed
Futura Display

Impact
Impressum
Impressum Bold
* Imprint
* Imprint Bold

Janson
Janson Italic
Jenson Old Style
Joanna
Joanna Italic
JOCUNDA *

Kabel Light
Kabel Medium
Kabel Bold
Kabel Bold Condensed
Kabel Heavy
Koloss Condensed
Korinna
Korinna Bold

USC Hawley
Lightline Gothic
LINCOLN GOTHIC
Litho Light Roman

Optima
Optima Italic
Optima Medium
Optima Semi-Bold
Optima Bold
Optima Ultra Bold

Mellor
Mellor Italic
Mellor Semi-Bold
Mellor Bold
Mellor Bold Condensed
Mellor Bold Radiant
Meridien Semi-Bold
* Million
Modern N°20
Modern N°20 Italic
MOORE COMPUTER

Sabon
Sabon Semi-Bold *
Schadow Antiqua Bold
Schneidler Old Style
Schneidler Old Style Bold *

Serif Gothic
Serif Gothic Bold

Shield
Skylark
Snell Roundhand
Souvenir Light
Souvenir Light Italic
Souvenir Medium
Souvenir Medium Italic
Souvenir Demi-Bold
Souvenir Demi-Bold Italic
Souvenir Bold
Souvenir Bold Italic
Sphinx
Standard Bold
Step *
STEELPLATE GOTHIC BOLD
Stymie Light
Stymie Medium
Stymie Bold
Stymie Extra Bold

Neptune
News Gothic
News Gothic Condensed
News Gothic Extra Condensed
News Gothic Bold
Novel Gothic

Tempo Heavy Condensed
Tempo Black
Tempo Black Condensed
THEATRE *
Times New Roman
Times New Roman Italic
Times New Roman Italic Semi-Bold
Times New Roman Semi-Bold
Times Roman Bold
Times Bold Modified N°1
Times Bold Modified N°2
Torino
Torino Italic

Pabst Black
Palatino
Palatino Italic
Palatino Medium
Palatino Semi-Bold
Palatino Bold
Parsons
Parsons Bold
Pascal
Perpetua
Perpetua Italic
Perpetua Bold
Plantin Light 113
Plantin Light 113 Italic
Plantin 110

Plantin 110 Italic
Plantin Bold
Plantin Bold Italic
Plantin Bold Condensed
Plantin Bold Condensed Outline
Plantin Extra Bold Condensed *
Players *
Poor Richard
Pretorian *

Radiant Medium
Radiant Bold
Radiant Heavy
RAILROAD GOTHIC
Rockwell Light
Rockwell Medium
Rockwell Bold
Romana
Romana Bold

Weiss Roman
Weiss Roman Bold
Weiss Roman Extra Bold
Westminster *
Windsor Light Condensed
Windsor
Windsor Outline
Williams Sans Medium *
Worcester Round
Worcester Round Italic *
Worcester Round Medium *
Worcester Round Bold *

Verona
Verona Italic
Verona Bold
Veronese *
Veronese Semi-Bold
Veronese Bold *
Vista
Vivaldi

Univers Light 45(685)
Univers Medium 55(689)
Univers Medium Condensed 57(690)
Univers Bold 65(693)
Univers Bold Condensed 67(694)
Univers Extra Bold 75(696)

Exclusively designed typefaces marked * are protected by copyright and subject to royalty. Typefaces marked • are generally unobtainable and have been selectively chosen to improve the standard range.

2

ABCDEFG
HIJKLMNO
PQRSTUV
WXYZ ŒÆ
1234567890

ABCDEF
GHIIJKLL
MNOPQR
SSTTUV
WXYZ.

1
2
4
6

WINDSOR ULTRA HEAVY

ABCDEFGHIJK
LMNOPQRST
UVWXYZ
abcdefghijklmno
pqrstuvwxyz
1234567890
&?!£$

E1 E1 Eal
a a

FRIZ QUADRATA BOLD

ABCDEFGHI
JKLMNOPQRSTUV
WXYZ
abcdefghijklm
nopqrstuvwxyz
1234567890
&?!£$

E1 E1 Eal
a a

AMERICAN TYPEWRITER BOLD CONDENSED

ABCDEFGHIJKL
MNOPQRST
UVWXYZ
abcdefghijklmn
opqrstuvwxyz
1234567890
&?!£$

E1 E1 Eal
a a

MELLISSA INLINE

AABBCDDEEFFG
HHIIJJKKLLMMNNO
PPQQRRSSTTU
UVVVWWW
XYYZZ
abcdefghh.ijkk.lmm.n
n.opqrrstuvwxy.yzz
1234567890&?!£$

E1 E1 Eal
a a

History has given us certain graphic classics that we hold in high respect not only for their dateless artistic charm, but for their continuing power to stimulate and motivate.

In typographic circles Bookman is one of these classics but, like the brownstone, the time finally comes

when it needs a thorough renovation to be useful to us here and now. Modern presses, modern papers, new ways to set type, new ease of kerning, tighter fit, contemporary weights – these are but a few of the important tools that have become commonplace since Bookman's first appearance years ago.

When Ed Benguiat undertook the task of updating Bookman, he did so with complete respect for the integrity of its original design. With perceptive discretion he intensified the classic flavor, at the same time moulding into the shapes those important typographical niceties that would

bring Bookman back to its rightful place in the graphic mainstream.

It is of considerable significance to note that while the original Bookman text typeface has heretofore been available only in one weight of roman and oblique, the new ITC Bookman has been designed in four weights –

3

abcccdefghijklmmnn
opqrsttuuvwwxyz
1234567890

5

אבגדהוזחטיכךלמםנוסעפףצץקרשת
1234567890

7

8

Typefaces
Caractères
Schrifttypen

1 Germany
AD/DES Wolf Magin
'Black Line': Experimenta Litera'

2 Canada
AD Government of Ontario
AG Case Associates
DIR John Cruikshank
DES Robert Burns
alphabet to identify public transit systems

3 Italy
AD Mecanorma
DES Nicola Russo
Instant lettering alphabet, neo prisma

4 Great Britain
Letraset (U.K.)
DES Studioteam
new alphabets

5 United States
AG Lanny Sommese Design
DES Lanny Sommese
typeface designed for moire effect

6 United States
AD ITC Photolettering Inc.
DES Edward Benguiat
Bookman

7 Israel
AD Art/Letraset-Israel
DES Dan Tel-Vardi
new Hebrew typeface

8 Great Britain
DES Richard Ward
new typeface alphabet for children

82-83

1a–b

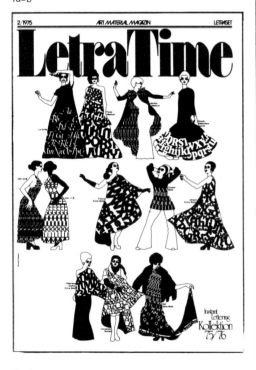

5a–b

Hollenstein Phototypo   Tél. 203.02.12
86, avenue du Président-Wilson
93210 Plaine St-Denis

alphabets créés et dessinés
en exclusivité pour
la collection Hollenstein par

2

3 b

3a

4

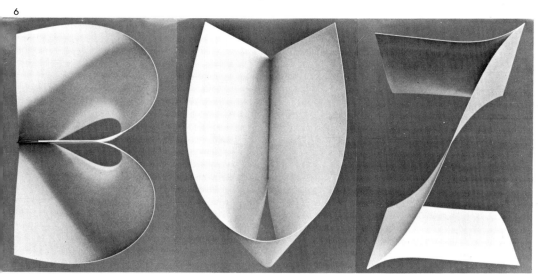

6

7

**Typefaces
Caractères
Schrifttypen**

1a-b Germany
AD Deutsche Letraset GmbH
DES Christof Gassner
COPY (a) Günther Kopp, Ulrike Feller
(b) Günther Kopp, Reinhold Jakob, Ulrike
Feller
instant lettering

2 France
AD Hollenstein
AG Hollenstein-phototypo
DIR Martin Reichen
DES Jean Larcher
phototype

3a-b United States
AD Photo Lettering Inc.
DES Stephen Kopec
(a) 'Star Spangled' series
(b) optical effects

4 Union of Soviet Socialist Republics
AD Publishing House Kunst/Tallin
DES Villu Toots
calligraphic studies

5 France
AD Mecanorma
AG Service Graphique
DIR Mr. Cayre
DES Cayre, Legendre
ILL M. Matussiere
instant lettering

6 Italy
AD Zucchi
AG Studio Coppola
DIR/DES Silvio Coppola
ILL Fotolight, Milano

7 France
AD Mecanorma
AG Service Graphique
DIR Mr Cayre
DES Cayre, Legendre
ILL M. Matussiere
Normasign (dépliant)

1

2

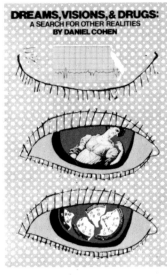

3

4

8

9

10

10a–b

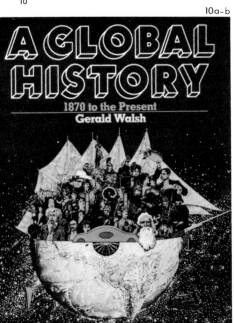

VÉRNÁSZ

Federico García Lorca

Pearl S. Buck
NOBELPREISTRÄGERIN
Letzte große Liebe
roro

5

6

7

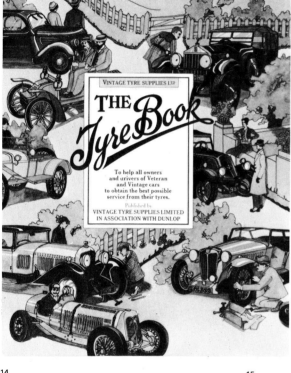

VINTAGE TYRE SUPPLIES LTD
THE Tyre Book
To help all owners
and drivers of Veteran
and Vintage cars
to obtain the best possible
service from their tyres.
Published by
VINTAGE TYRE SUPPLIES LIMITED
IN ASSOCIATION WITH DUNLOP

12

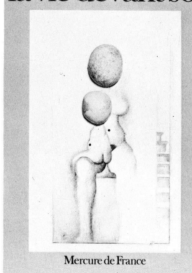

Emile Ajar
la vie devant soi

Mercure de France

13

14

15

MICHÈLE RICHARD
Gouverner
sa maison
sans y avoir
été
préparée

HACHETTE

Los Tlacuilos de Fray Diego Durán

Prólogo y Textos de Gonzalo Obregón
Edición privada de Cartón y Papel de México, S.A.
México 1975

1 Germany
AD Deutsche Verlags-Anstalt Stuttgart
DES Dieter Zembsch

2 Germany
AD C. Bertelsmann Verlag
DES Dieter Zembsch

3 United States
AD Franklin Watts Inc.
DIR Judi Mills
DES Frances Jetter

4 United States
AD Little, Brown and Co.
AG Wendell Minor Design
DIR Char Lappan
DES Wendell Minor

5 Brazil
AD Circulo do Livro S.A.
DES Alfredo Aquino

6 Hungary
AD Magyar Helikon
DES Tibor Szántó

7 Germany
AD Rowohlt Taschenbuch Verlag
DES Kirsti Marx

8 Great Britain
AD Thorsons Publishers
DES Tad Aronowicz

9 Italy
AD Arnoldo Mondadori Editore
DIR Bruno Binosi
DES Ferruccio Bocca

10 Brazil
AD Editora Nova Fronteira
AG Casa do Desenho
DIR/DES Raul Rangel Filho

11a-b Canada
AD Genny Goldberg
AG McClelland & Stewart Ltd
DIR (a) Rene Zamic
    (b) Jim McLachlan
DES Rene Zamic
educational books

12 Great Britain
AD Vintage Tyre Supplies Ltd
AG Tyrell Keeble Associates
DIR/DES Chris Keeble
ILL Jane Seager

13 France
AD Mercure de France
DES/ILL André François

14 France
AD Hachette
AG Primart
DIR Ulrich Meyer
DES Agnès Molnar

15 Mexico
AD/AG Carton y Papei
de Mexico S.A.

Bookjackets
Chemises de livres
Buchumschläge

1 Switzerland
AD Verlag Bohem Press
DES George Konetschny
ILL Jan Jedlicka

2a-b Hungary
DES László Réber

3 United States
AD Parent's Magazine Press
ILL Anne Rockwell

4 United States
AD/AG Pantheon Books
ILL Leo Lionni

5 United States
AD/AG Charles Scribner's Sons
ILL Jose Aruego, Ariane Dewey

6 Holland
AD/AG A. W. Bruna & Zoon, Utrecht
ILL Clara Marot

7 Israel
AD Sifriot Hapoalim
DES Shmuel Katz

8 Great Britain
AD/AG Dobson Books Ltd
ILL Marcello Minale (7 yrs)

9 Switzerland
AD/AG Atlantis Verlag Zurich and Freiburg
ILL Katrin Brandt

10 Germany
AD Bertelsmann Verlag
ILL Ulrik Schramm

11a-b Great Britain
AD/AG Jonathan Cape
ILL Nicola Bayley

12 France
AD/AG Librarie Classique, Eugene Belin
ILL Gerda Müller

1

2

5

7

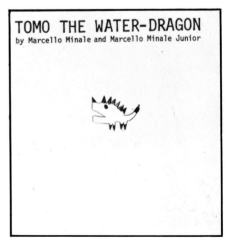

8

2b

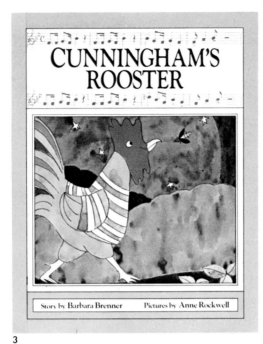

3

4

9

10

11a—b

12

1

2 a-b

6

7

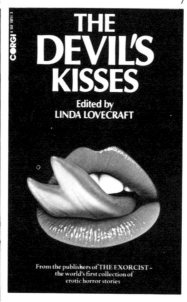

8

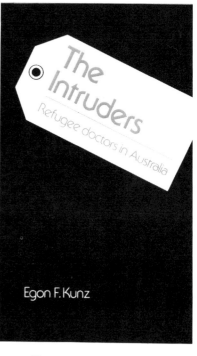

9

10

11

12

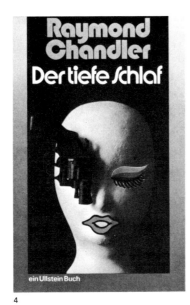

3

4

5

13

14

15a-b

Bookjackets
Chemises de livres
Buchumschläge

1 Germany
AD C. Bertelsmann
DES Dieter Zembsch

2a-b Spain
AD Circulo de Lectores, S.A.
DES Javier Noguera

3 Italy
AD Arnoldo Mondadori Editore
AG Servizio Grafico Editoriale
DIR Bruno Binosi
DES Ferenc Pintér

4 Germany
AD Verlag Ullstein
AG Peter Steiner
DIR Hans Roachim Reich
DES Peter Steiner

5 Australia
AD Macmillan Australia
DES Jack Larkin

6 Germany
AD Fischer Taschenbüch Verlag
DES Jan Buchholz, Reni Hinsch

7 Great Britain
AD Transworld Publishers Ltd (Corgi Books)
DIR John Munday
DES Steve Lang
ILL Chris Moore, Michael Morris

8 Australia
AD Australian National University
AG ANU Graphic Design
DIR/DES Stephen Cole

9 United States
AD Vintage Books (Random House Inc)
AG Wendell Minor Design
DIR Judy Loeser
DES Wendell Minor

10 Italy
AD Arnoldo Mondadori Editore
AG Servizio Grafico Editoriale
DIR Bruno Binosi
DES Ferenc Pintér

11 United States
AD J. B. Lippincott Co.
AG Wendell Minor Design
DIR Jean Krulis
DES Wendell Minor

12 Denmark
AD Gyldendal (publishers)
AG Gyldendal design
DIR/DES Austin Grandjean

13 Great Britain
AD Transworld Publishers
DIR/DES Roger Hammond
ILL Brian Sweet

14 Germany (DDR)
DES Peter Nagengast

15a-b Great Britain
AD Weidenfeld & Nicolson
DIR (a) Behram Kapadia, (b) James Campus
DES (a) James Campus, (b) Nick Sutton
ILL (a) Jules Feiffer

1

2

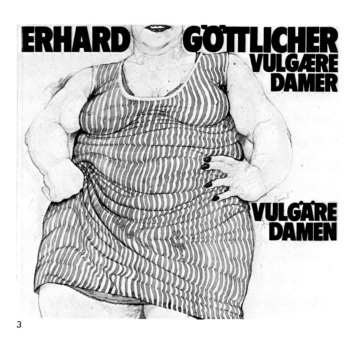

3

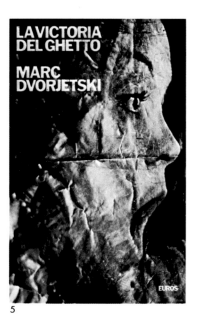

5

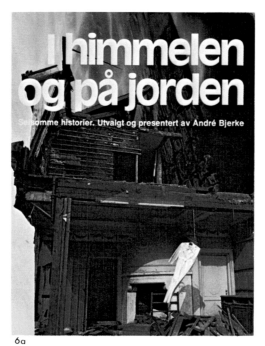

6a

6b

7a–b–c

4a–b–c

8a–b

9

10

11

1 Great Britain
AD W. H. Allen & Co. Ltd
DIR John Munday
DES Roman Buj

2 Great Britain
AD W. H. Allen
AG Roman & Moira Buj
DIR John Munday
DES Roman Buj

3 Germany
AD Erhard Göttlicher
ILL Erhard Göttlicher

4a-c Great Britain
AD Fontana Books
DIR/DES (a,b) Tad Aronowicz
       (c) Mike Dempsey
ILL (c) Sally Patch

5 Spain
AD Euros
AG C. Rolando & Asociados
DIR/DES C. Rolando, R. Dosil
ILL Daniel Campo

6a-b Norway
AD Den Norske Bokklubben
ILL Beth Toming

7a-c France
AD Librarie Belin
AG Atelier de creation Belin
DIR Mario Pasini
DES (a) Michele Fraudreau,
     (b) Roselyne Ballereau
     (c) Mario Pasini
ILL (a) Martin Fraudreau,
     (b) R. W. Martin,
     (c) Ivan Massar (Rapho)

8a-b Great Britain
AD Penguin
AG Pentagram
DIR/DES Mervyn Kurlansky

9 Italy
AD Arnoldo Mondadori Editore
DIR Bruno Binosi
DES Ferruccio Bocca

10 Great Britain
AD Weidenfeld & Nicolson
DIR/DES Behram Kapadia

11 Great Britain
AD W. H. Allen
DIR John Munday
DES Val Biro
ILL Stanli Oppermann

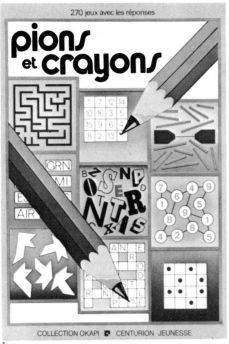

1

2

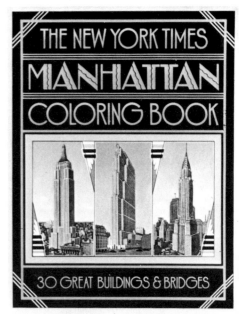

3

6

9

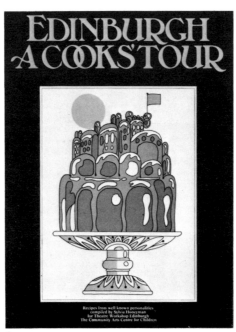

7

10

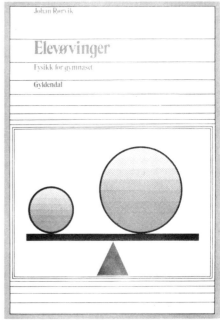

8

11

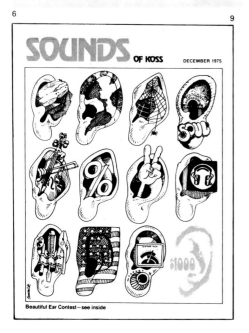

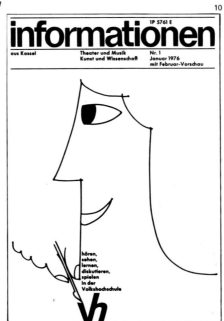

Indian Art Direction
The Magazine of
Graphic Communication
Inaugural Issue
October 1975

4

5

1 France
AD Centurion Jeunesse
AG Okapi
DIR Denys Prache
DES France de Ranchin

2 United States
AD Simon & Schuster
AG Barnett /Goslin/Barnett

3 United States
AD/AG Quadrangle, The New York Times Book
Company
ILL David Edward Byrd

4 India
AD Indian Art Direction
DIR Aravind Teki
DES Man Mohan

5 Japan
AD Yomiuri Newspaper Office
DIR/DES Tadanori Yokoo

6 Italy
AD Linea Grafica
DES Rinaldo Cutini

7 Italy
AD Progresso Grafico
AG Studio Giob
DIR/DES R. del Sordo
ILL B. Garavoglia

8 Norway
AD/AG Gyldendal Norsk Forlag
DES Gunnar Lilleng

9 United States
AD Koss Steriophones
AG Advertising Art Studio Inc
DIR John Lowin
DES John Constable

10 Germany
AD Magistrat Kassel
DES Reinhard Matthäus

11 Great Britain
AD Theatre Workshop Edinburgh
AG Forth Studios Ltd
DIR/DES Andrew Hunter
ILL James Gorman
COPY Murray Sladen
arts centre for children

12 Poland
AD 'Pagart' — Polish artists' agency
DES J. Rafal Olbinski
international song festival

13 Germany
AD German Federal Government
DES Heinz Bähr

14 Poland
AD 'Poland' — Illustrated magazine
DIR Lech Zahorski
DES Adam Kilian

12

13

14

Postage Stamp Designs
Dessins de Timbres-poste
Briefmarken-Entwürfe

1 United States
AG Postal Service
DES Vincent E. Hoffman

2 Gibraltar
DES A. G. Ryamm
Bicentennial

3 Jersey
AD Department of Postal Administration
DES M. D. Orbell

4 United States
AG Postal Service
DES Walt Reed

5 Bahamas
AG Crown Agents
DES Waddington Studio

6 Norfolk Island
AG Crown Agents
DES Harrison & Sons Ltd

7 Israel
AD Ministry of Posts-Philatelic Service
DES Adrian Lucaci
Bicentennial

8 Gambia
AG Crown Agents
DES Clive Abbott

9 Isle of Man
AG John Waddington of Kirkstall Ltd
Bicentennial

10 Pitcairn Islands
AG Crown Agents
DES Jennifer Toombs
Bicentennial

11 Tchad
DES M. Gauthier

12 France
AD Direction Poste et Télécommunication
DES R. Quilliric

13 Cayman Islands
AG Crown Agents
DES P. B. Powell
Bicentennial

14 Eire
DES Louis le Brocquy
Bicentennial

15 Virgin Islands
AG Crown Agents
DES John Waddington Studio

16 Norway
AG Postens
Filatelitjenete
DES Sverre Morken

17a-e Canada
AD Canadian Post Office
DES (a,b) Jean Mercier
    (c,d) Ray Webber
    (e) Allan R. Fleming
Montreal Olympics

18 Germany (DDR)
AD Postministerium
DES Joachim Riess
DDR Olympics

1

2

3

4

5

6

7

The Gambia
50B
Continental Army
Bicentennial of American Independence

8

E II R
AMERICAN REVOLUTION
BICENTENNIAL 1776-1976
13p
COL. PATRICK HENRY · FIRST VIRGINIA REGIMENT
ISLE OF MAN
WADDINGTON 1976

9

E II R
AMERICAN REVOLUTION
BICENTENNIAL 1776-1976
7p
THE VIRGINIA GAZETTE
WILLIAM CHRISTIE CARRYING THE PROCLAMATION TO WILLIAMSBURG
ISLE OF MAN
WADDINGTON 1976

U.S. BI-CENTENNIAL 1776
50c
'Mayflower'
Pitcairn Islands

10

U.S. BI-CENTENNIAL 1776
30c
George Washington
Pitcairn Islands

RÉPUBLIQUE DU TCHAD   POSTE AERIENNE
200
150F
1776. FONDATION DES ÉTATS-UNIS D'AMÉRIQUE

11

BICENTENAIRE DE L'INDEPENDANCE DES ETATS-UNIS
1776 1976
1.20
FRANCE POSTES
VERGENNES   FRANKLIN

12

CAYMAN ISLANDS
HOPE
20c

13

EIRE
7
American Declaration of Independence 1776

14

EIRE
8
American Declaration of Independence 1776

SALUTE TO U.S. BI-CENTENNIAL
British Virgin Islands
40c
CONTINENTAL NAVY FRIGATE RALEIGH
WADDINGTON STUDIO   1976   QUESTA

15

UTVANDRINGEN TIL AMERIKA
NORGE
1.25
S. MORKEN 1975

16

olympiade olympiad
Montréal 1976
Canada
$1

Canada
$2
olympiade olympiad
XXI
Montréal 1976

17 a – b

Olympiade XXI Olympiad Montréal 1976
Canada 25

17 c – d

Olympiade XXI Olympiad Montréal 1976
Canada 50

Canada $2
R. Tait McKenzie MD
sculptor/sculpteur
Olympiade XXI Olympiad Montréal 1976

17 e

18

KLEINE FRIEDENSFAHRT
5
DDR
SPIELE DER XXI. OLYMPIADE 1976

10+5
DDR
DHfK-SCHWIMMHALLE LEIPZIG
SPIELE DER XXI. OLYMPIADE 1976

70
DDR
MEILENLAUF
SPIELE DER XXI. OLYMPIADE 1976

1a–b

2a–b–c

3a–b

4

5a–b–c

6

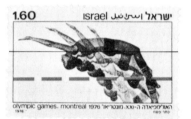

7

8

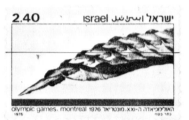

10

14a–b

11a–b

9

13

12

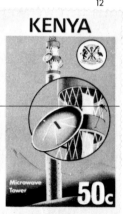

15

16

17

18

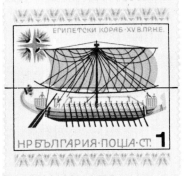

19

20

1a-b Liechtenstein
AD Government of the Principate
DES Louis Jaeger

2a-d Monaco
AD/AG Principauté de Monaco — Poste
et Télécommunications
DES (a) P. Forget, (b) J. Gauthier,
(C) R. Quilliric,

3a-b Samoa
AG Crown Agents
DES Clive Abbott

4 Bhutan
AD Department of Posts
AG Inter-Governmental Philatelic Corp.
DES Waddington Studio
Innsbruck Olympics

5a-c Israel
AD Ministry of Communication
DES D. Pessah, S. Ketter
Montreal Olympics

6 Malta
AD Philatelic Bureau, General Post Office
DES Harry Alden

7 Monaco
AD Postes et Télécommunications
DES P. Forget
telephone centenary

8 Brazil
AD Empresa Brasileira de Correios e Telegrafos
DES M. Carmem Ferreira
telephone centenary

9 Brazil
AD Empresa de Correios e Telegrafos
DES C. Calvi
Interamerican Telecommunications Conference

10 Luxemburg
AG Administration des Postes
DES R. Domseiffer
Olympics

11 a-b Switzerland
AG Schweizerische PTT Wertzeichenabteilung
DES (a) Walter Beutter,
(B) Aldred Cserno, Jean-Jacques Chevally
(a) Helping Hand, (b) Telephone centenary

12 Portugal
DES Jose Candido
Telephone centenary

13 Israel
AD Ministry of Communication
DES Asher Kalderon
satellite communication

14 New Hebrides
AG Crown Agents
DES M. Gauthier, Paris
ILL Delrieu

15 Kenya
AG Crown Agents

21a

21b

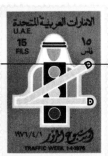

21c

22a–b

23

24

25

26

16 Malawi
AG Crown Agents
DES Clive Abbott
Telephone centenary

17 Mexico
DES R. Davidson
Telephone centenary

18 Belgium
DES M. Severin
Antwerp Zoo

19 Bulgaria
AD Ministry of Communications
DES Stephen Kantscheff

20 Austria
AD Bundesministerium für den Verkehr
DES W. Swidel
modern Austrian art

21a-c Switzerland
DES (a,b) Celestino Piatti,
(C) André Rosselet
(a) prevention of leprosy
(b) help for the handicapped
(c) forest conservation

22a-b Swaziland
AG Crown Agents
DES Jennifer Toombs
prevention of blindness

23 United Arab Emirate
AG Crown Agents
DES Mohamed Samood
traffic week

24 Holland
AG Netherlands Postal Service
DES P. Patiwal, Gratama. de Vries
and Van der Toorn Partnership

25 Sri Lanka
AG Crown Agents
DES P. Wanigatuna

26 Australia
AD Australian Post
AG Stamps and Philatelic Branch
DES R. Ingpen
pioneer life

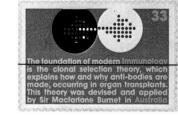
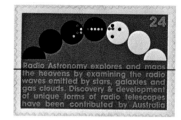

1a-b-c-d

2a

2b

2c

2d

2e

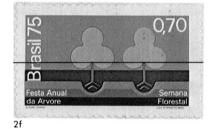

2f

2g

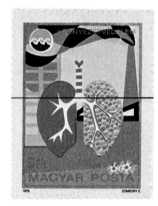

3a-b-c-d

4a-b-c-d

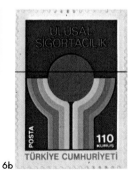

5a-b-c

6a

6b

7a-b-c

7d

7g

7e-f

7i

7j

7h

1a-d Australia
AD Australian Postal Commission
AG Stamps and Philatelic Branch
DIR Chairman, Stamp Advisory Committee
DES Bruce Weatherhead, Alex Stitt

2a-g Brazil
AD Empresa Brasileira Correios e Telégrafos
AG (b,c,d) Casado Desenho
DES (a,e) Ary Fagundes,
    (b,c,d) Gian Calvi,
    (f) Suzanna D'Arinos,
    (g) Maria Carmem Ferreira

3a-d Hungary
AD Hungarian Post Office
DES Eva Zombory

4a-d New Zealand
AD N.Z. Post Office
DES A. P. Derrick

5a-c Jersey
AD Department of Postal Administration
AG Crown Agents
DES Abram Games
tourism

6a-b Turkey
AD General Directorate of PTT
DES (a) Mengü Ertel,
    (b) Yurdaer Altintas
(a) nationalisation of insurance organisations
(b) fine arts

7a-j Israel
AD (a-h,j) Ministry of Posts-Philatelic Service
    (i) UN Postal Administration
DES (a,b,c) E. Weishoff, (d) M. Felheim,
    (e,f) O. E. Schwarz, (g,i) Asher Kalderon,
    (h) M. Pereg, (j) A. Hecht
(a,b,c,) pollution
(d) camping
(e,f,g) festival
(h) border settlements
(i) air mail
(j) academy

8a-d Malta
AD General Post Office
AG Philatelic Bureau, General Post Office
DES Nazareno Camilleri
customs and traditions

9 Fiji
AG Crown Agents
DES Jennifer Toombs
festival

10 Finland
AD Suomen Posti-ja Lennätinhallitus
DES Pentti Rahikainen
(a) 500th Anniversary of St Olaf Castle
(b) European conference on security and
cooperation

11 Italy
DES L. M. Boschini
World Philatelic Exhibition

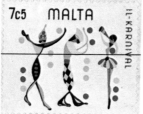

8a-b-c-d

9

10b

10a

11

International Women's Year
Eleanor Roosevelt

Seychelles RS 3.50

1

سلطنة عمان
SULTANATE OF OMAN
POSTAGE
عام المرأة العالمي ١٩٧٥
INTERNATIONAL WOMEN'S YEAR 1975
150 BAIZA ١٥٠

2

International Women's Year 1975
40c
ST CHRISTOPHER-NEVIS-ANGUILLA
Marie Curie – discoverer of radium

3

15c
WOMEN IN CRAFTS
SWAZILAND

4

1975
ANNÉE INTERNATIONALE DE LA FEMME
RÉPUBLIQUE DU DAHOMEY
50f

5

INTERNATIONAL WOMEN'S YEAR 1975
AUSTRALIA 10

6

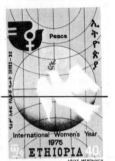

Peace
International Women's Year 1975
ETHIOPIA 40c
ABIYE MEKONNEN

Equality
International Women's Year 1975
ETHIOPIA 90c
ABIYE MEKONNEN

7a–b

POSTES ANNÉE FRANCE INTERNATIONALE DE LA FEMME
1975 · 1.20

8

35
JAAR VAN DE VROUW
NEDERLAND
35

9

Helvetia 30
1975 Jahr der Frau Année de la femme Anno della donna
HANS ERNI   COURVOISIER S.A.

10

10c
INTERNATIONAL WOMEN'S YEAR 1975
SINGAPORE EQUALITY

35c
INTERNATIONAL WOMEN'S YEAR 1975
SINGAPORE DEVELOPMENT

75c
INTERNATIONAL WOMEN'S YEAR 1975
SINGAPORE PEACE

11a–b–c

NORGE 125
FNS KVINNEÅR 1975

12

Tahun Wanita Internasional 1975
40,
REPUBLIK INDONESIA

13

1.20
MONACO ANNÉE INTERNATIONALE DE LA FEMME
1975

14

Brasil 75 3,30
ANO INTERNACIONAL DA MULHER MARTHA POPPE

15

1945 – 1975 10c
UNITED NATIONS NATIONS UNIES
THE HOPE OF MANKIND
NACIONES UNIDAS
объединенные нации

16

السنة الدولية للمرأة ١٩٧٥
POSTAGE
INTERNATIONAL WOMEN'S 1975
15 FILS STATE of KUWAIT
دولة الكويت

17

MALTA
IS-SENA INTERNAZZJONALI TAN-NISA
1975
20c

18

MALAYSIA 15c
TAHUN WANITA ANTARABANGSA 1975

19

GUYANA 50 CENTS
INTERNATIONAL WOMEN'S YEAR 1975

20

12P

52nd Inter-Parliamentary Conference

21a

Jane Austen 1775-1817 Catherine Morland 10P

Jane Austen 1775-1817 Mary and Henry Crawford 13P

21b–c

1 Seychelles
AG Crown Agents
DES Clive Abbott
International Women's Year

2 Oman
AG Crown Agents
DES PAD Studio
Women's Year

3 St Christopher, Nevis, Anguilla
AG Crown Agents
DES Jennifer Toombs
Women's Year

4 Swaziland
AG Crown Agents
DES J.-J. Rostami
Women's Year

5 Dahomey
DES N. Delange
Women's Year

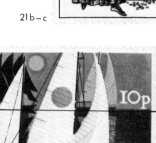

8p

10p

12p

21d–e–f

6 Australia
AD Australia Post (Australian Postal Commission)
AG Stamps and Philatelic Branch
DIR Chairman, Stamps Advisory Committee
DES Leonora Howlett
Women's Year

Stephenson's Locomotion 7P

Caerphilly Castle 10P

High-Speed Train 12P

1825 Stockton and Darlington Railway

1923 Great Western Railway Castle Class

1975 British Rail Inter-City Service HST

21g–h–i

7a-b Ethiopia
AD Provisional Military Govt of Socialist Ethiopia
AG Ministry of Transport and Communications
    Ethiopian Postal Service
DES Ato Abiy Mekonnen
Women's Year

8 France
AD Direction Poste et Télécommunication
DES G. Lacroix
Women's Year

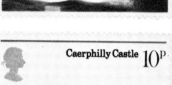

7p

7p Charlotte Square Edinburgh

12p

21j–k–l

9 Holland
AD/AG Netherlands Postal Service
DES Ans Bockting-van Genderen
Women's Year

10 Switzerland
AG Schweizerische PTT Wertzeichenabteilung
DES Hans Erni
Women's Year

22

11a-c Singapore
AG Crown Agents
DES Tay Sien Chiah
Women's Year

12 Norway
AD Direction Générale des Postes
AG Postens Filatelitjeneste
DES Ingrid Jangaard Onsland

13 Indonesia
AD/AG Directorate General of Posts
DES Suprapto Martosuhardjo
Women's Year

14 Monaco
AD/AG Postes et Télécommunications

15 Brazil
AD Empreisa Brasileira de Correios
DES Martha Poppe
Women's Year

16 Israel
AD UNPA
DES Asher Kalderon
Women's Year

17 Kuwait
AD/AG Ministry of Communication
Women's Year

18 Malta
AD General Post Office
AG Philatelic Bureau, General Post Office
DES Donald Friggieri
Women's Year

19 Malaysia
AD Malaysian Advertising Services
AG Crown Agents
Women's Year

20 Guyana
AG Crown Agents
DES PAD Studio
Women's Year

21a-l Great Britain
AD British Post Office
DIR Stuart Rose
DES (a, b) Meffery Matthews,
    (c) Richard Downer, (d-f) Andrew Restall,
    (g-i) John Ward, (J-l) Peter Gauld

22 Bulgaria
AD Ministry of Communications
AG Bulgarian Post Office
Christmas stamps

23 a-c Norway
AG Postens Filatelitjeneste
DES (a) S. Morken
    (b-c) Henry Welde

23 a–c

UTVANDRINGEN TIL AMERIKA

NORGE 1.40

MAGNUS LAGABØTERS LANDSLOV 1274

NORGE 1.00

MAGNUS LAGABØTERS LANDSLOV 1274

NORGE 1.40

Trademarks,
Letterheads,
Co-ordinated design

1

3a–b

2

1 United States
AD The Communications Counsel of America
AG The Weller Institute
DIR/DES Don Weller
COPY Ron Gossling

2 Denmark
AD Södahl Design A/S
AG Finn Hjernøe's Grafiske Tegnestue
DES Finn Hjernøe
USA jubilee trademark

3a-b United States
AD Pepsi-Cola Company
AG Pepsi-Cola Graphic Arts Dept
DIR/DES Sondra Scarzafava
(a) bottler's convention
(b) American freedom train celebrating
bicentennial

4 Australia
AD/AG Grey Advertising Ltd
DIR/DES Tony Stewart
stationery,

Grey Advertising Pty. Ltd.

What you said to Grey Advertising and what we said to you.

Another memo.

The words for an ad from Grey Advertising.

Job No.

Client.

Medium.

Date.

What your next television commercial from Grey Advertising should cost you.

Client:

Product:

Description:

Length:

A breakdown of our costs.

Client:

Product:

Length:

Date:

Key No.:

On air date:

Breakdown of other production expenses:

Pilot conception work: $

Pre-testing: $

Storyboard: $

Artwork: $

TV Packs: $

Still Photography: $

Screen tests: $

A parcel from Grey Advertising.

With compliments from Grey Advertising.

21 Grosvenor Street, Neutral Bay, 2089. Tel. 909-3999.
P.O. Box 294, Neutral Bay Junction, 2089. N.S.W. Australia.

A letter from Grey Advertising.

An airmail letter from Grey Advertising.

An official instruction to place this material from Grey Advertising.

2002

Publication: Date:

Client: Product:

Date: Size: Key/caption: Material: Position: P/line:

Why Grey Advertising are giving you money.

Remittance advice for the month of   19

To:

An order for time or space from Grey Advertising.

Reference No.:   Issued:

The Advertising Manager:

A credit note from Grey Advertising.

Client:

Product: Medium:

Date of insertion or broadcast:

Details of cost:

Everything you need to start a job.

Client: Date:

Division: Product:

Account Executive: Job No.:

Job Description

Brief:

A.E. brief to traffic: Final Media deadline:

Press/Print: Copy required:

Layout required:

Revised copy/layout required:

Finished Art required:

Revised Finished Art required:

Radio: Script required:

Revised Script required:

Final tape required:

Television: Script required:

Storyboard required:

Revised script/storyboard required:

Double head required:

Answer print required:

Research: Concepts required:

Concept cards required:

Talk back required:

1

1 United States
AD The Wurlitzer Company
AG The Design Partnership
DIR Jack Weiss
DES Les Holloway
ILL Katherine Fulton
COPY Victor Zast
music merchant

2 Great Britain
AD Speedy Cartoons
AG Robin Bath Design
DIR Paul Vester
DES Robin Bath
animation group

2

5

5 Great Britain
AD ICI Offshore
AG ICI Publicity Services
DIR D. A. Pratt
DES H. Potter
exploration of North Sea oil

6 Germany
AD Lutz Roeder
AG Apollon
DIR/DES Lutz Roeder
art director's promotion

6

9

9 France
AD Barved Zumizion
DES Jean Larcher
audio-visual society

10 Great Britain
AD TFC Foods Ltd
AG Eurographics Ltd
frozen food distributor, distributeur du congelé

10

RAINIER BANK

13

13 United States
AD Rainier National Bank
AG Lippincott & Margulies Inc.
DES Frank Delano
bank

14 Peru
AD Le Bouquet Garni
DES Claude Dieterich
restaurant

14

17

17 Spain
AD Union de Acústica y Sonido S.A.
AG Studio Ariño
DES Pere Ariño
hi-fi

18 Austria
AD Sveda
AG Watzlwork
DIR/DES Peter Watzl
central heating, chauffage central,
Zentralheizung

18

3

3 Great Britain
AD Radford Hifi Ltd
AG Ron Ellis Design
DIR/DES Ron Ellis
hi-fi

4 France
AD Les Files de Fourmies
AG Graphic & Co.
DIR F. Schweblin
DES P. Courivaud

4

7

7 Australia
AD Expression Pty Ltd
DES Stephan Cole
do-it-yourself picture framing system,
Encadrement de tableaux, Bilderrahmen

8 Belgium
AD Radiodiffusion Télévision Belge
DES Jacques Richez
TV

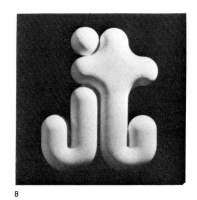

8

11

11 Great Britain
AD Star, Milan, Italy
AG Minale, Tattersfield, Provinciali Ltd
food company

12 Italy
AD Executive Club
DES Rinaldo Cutini
club

12

15

15 Argentina
AD Hogartex S.A.
AG Oscar N. Marcovecchio S.A. de Publicidad
DIR Néstor O. Denis
ILL Guillermo Balboa
camping material

16 Germany
AD Imbiss-International
DES Erich Unger
restaurant chain

16

20

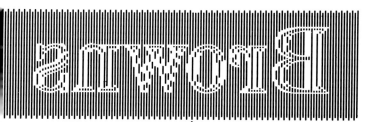

9

19 Great Britain
AD Browns Ltd
AG Minale, Tattersfield, Provinciali Ltd
textiles

20 Italy
AD Sacis
AG Studio Ruffolo
DIR/DES Sergio Ruffolo
television

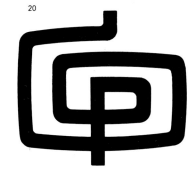

1 United States
AD Telephone Computing Service, Inc.
AG George Lowe Advertising
DIR/DES Ken Parkhurst
telephone bill-paying system, payment du
téléphone, Telefonbezahlung

2 United States
AD The National Association for Creative
Children and Adults
AG Lipson-Jacob Associates
DIR/DES Stan Brod

3 Germany
AD Melitta Groeben
DES Ronald Koob
chiropodist, pedicure

4 Canada
AD Oakville Harbour Commission
AG Burns & Cooper Ltd
DIR/DES Robert Burns
ILL Paul Walker

5 India
AD/AG Artcel
DIR/DES Binay Saha
communication design studio

6 Spain
AD Chiminord
AG Publis
DIR/DES Salvatore Adduci
silicones company

7 Germany
AD C. A. Froh
DES Peter Steiner
initials

8 Australia
AD Dynamic Leisure
AG Toplan Sales Promotion Pty Ltd
DIR/DES Frank Eidlitz
revolutionary new golf clubs

9 Peru
AD Editorial Ser
DES Claude Dieterich,
publisher, maison d'edition, Verleger

10 Mexico
AD Centro de Ciencias Educativas, Mexico City
AG Robin Bath Design
DIR Ricardo Ampudia
DES Robin Bath
education centre

11 Hong Kong
AD Creation House
AG 3A Publicity 'n Promotion
DIR/DES Michael Miller, Yu

12 Bulgaria
AD Committee for Television and Radio
DES Nikola Petrov Nikolov
sports department

13 France
AD Air France
AG Garamond
DIR R. C. Garamond
DES Jacques Nathan-Garamond
airline

14 Belgium
AD Ballet van Vlaanderen
AG Paul Ibou
ballet

15 Great Britain
AD Zuhair Fayes Associates, Saudi Arabia
AG Unit Five Design Ltd
DIR/DES Terry Tyrrell
architect

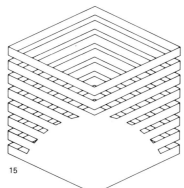

16 Canada
AD Owl Bar
AG Design Collaborative
DIR/DES Ernst Roch
bar

17 Canada
AD Creative Playgrounds
AG Burton Kramer Assoc. Ltd
DIR/DES Burton Kramer
playground and play equipment, matériel de
cour de récréation material für Sport und
Spielplatz

18 United States
AD Division Stampings Inc.
DES Cyril John Schlosser
metal stamping company, emboutisage,
Metallpresse

19 Japan
AD Central Studio
AG Japan Ad-Art, Inc.
DIR/DES Masahiro Oishi
photographic studio

20 Japan
AD Toko Electric Co. Ltd
AG Madison Ad. & Creative Agency
DIR/DES Eiichi Hasegawa

21 South Africa
AD Syrkel Theatre Group
AG Stilborg & Design
DIR/DES Beni Stilborg

22 Great Britain
AD Tyldesley Methodist Church
DES Anthony D. Forster
church, église, Kirche

23 Spain
AD Universidad Politécnica de Barcelona
DES Pere Ariño
symposium on education

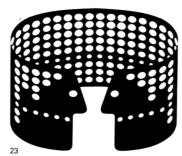

24 Italy
AD ETI Casavacanze
DES Giovanni Brunazzi
holiday homes, colonies de vacance,
Ferienkolonien

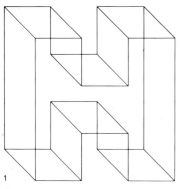

1 Great Britain
AD Hammerplast
AG Royle/Murgatroyd Design Assoc.
DIR Keith Murgatroyd
DES Anthony D. Forster
plexiglass products

2 Cuba
AD Ministerio de Transporte
DES Felix Beltran
taxis

3 Spain
AD 114 Furniture
AG 8ctav8
DIR/DES Perez Sanchez
furniture, meubles, Möbel

4 Canada
AD Excel Modular Wall Systems
AG Design Collaborative
DIR/DES Rolf Harder
modular wall systems, furniture

5 Israel
AD Kidis Kidswear
AG Zvi Karmon Advertising
DIR/DES Yak Molho
children's wear, vêtements d'enfants,
Kinderkleider

6 India
AD Council of Architecture
AG NID/HHEC/Design Cell
DIR/DES Benoy Sarkar

7 Spain
AD Hercofil
AG Soley/Torrecilla
DIR Santiago Soley, Miguel Torrecilla
DES Miguel Torrecilla

8 United States
AD International Harvester
AG BBDM Inc.
DIR/DES Michael Kelly
ILL Horst Mickler

9 United States
AD Environmental Equipment Leasing
Company
AG The Marketing Department
DIR/DES Bob Coonts

10 Israel
AD Yagev Ltd
DES Jacob Landau
agricultural supplies, fournitures agricoles,
Landwirtschaft material

11 Bulgaria
DES Stephan Kanscheff
cultural club

12 Austria
AD Bregenzer Festspiele
AG Vorarlberger Graphik
DES Othmar Motter
festival, Festspiele

13 Iran
DES Fouzi Tehrani
building constructions, constructions
immobilières, Hauskonstruktion

13

14

14 Canada
AD Canadian Association for a Clean
Environment
AG Design Collaborative
DIR/DES Ernst Roch
environmental

15 United States
AD James Harvey
AG The Design Partnership
DIR/DES Lindell Mabrey
initial

15

16 Bulgaria
AD Bulgarian Exhibition Stand
DES Stephan Kantscheff
Expo 75 for Oceanography

16

17 Canada
AD Canadian Lamp and Fixture Manufacturers
Association
AG John German Graphic Design
DIR/DES John German
lamps

17

18

18 Canada
AD Travel Fun Tours
AG Burton Kramer Assoc. Ltd
DIR/DES Burton Kramer
travel agency, agence de voyages, Reisebüro

19 South Africa
AD Nedsual Insurance Brokers (Pty) Ltd
AG Jeremy Sampson Associates
DIR/DES Jeremy Sampson
insurance, assurance, Versicherung

19

20 United States
AD Brever Electric Company
AG Edward Hughes Design
DIR/DES Edward Hughes
industrial vacuum cleaners, aspirateurs
industriels, Industrielle Staubsauger

Tornado

20

21

.1 Iran
AD Iranian Society of Export Accountants
AG/DIR Morteza Momayez
DES Mohammad Reza Adnani
accountants, contables, Buchsachverständiger

22 United States
AD Ram Ridge Corporate Park
DES Robert A. Gale
industrial estate

22

24 Iran
DES Barkeshlou Manssouri
society for health

24

23 Great Britain
AD Universal Signs
AG Ron Ellis Design
DIR/DES Ron Ellis
signwriters, peintres d'enseignes
Schildermahler

23

110-111

Trademarks
Marques
Schutzmarken

1 Canada
AD Calgary Stampede & Rodeo
AG Burns & Cooper Ltd
DIR Robert Burns
DES Roger Hill
ILL Roger Hill, Paul Walker

2a-c United States
AD Universal Oil Products
AG Robert Miles Runyan & Associates
DIR Robert Miles Runyan
DES Rusty Kay
oil refiners

3 United States
AD National Zoological Park
AG Wyman & Cannan Company
DIR/DES Lance Wyman, Bill Cannan
ILL Lance Wyman, Brian Flahive, Ernesto
Lehfeld
zoo

4a-c Great Britain
AD Whitbread & Co.
AG Derek Forsyth Graphics Ltd
DIR Derek Forsyth
DES Tim Dunnell
ILL Ian Taylor
beer, bière, Bier

Bareback Bronc Riding Chuckwagon Racing Bull Riding

Calf Roping Steer Wrestling Saddle Bronc Riding

1a–f

3

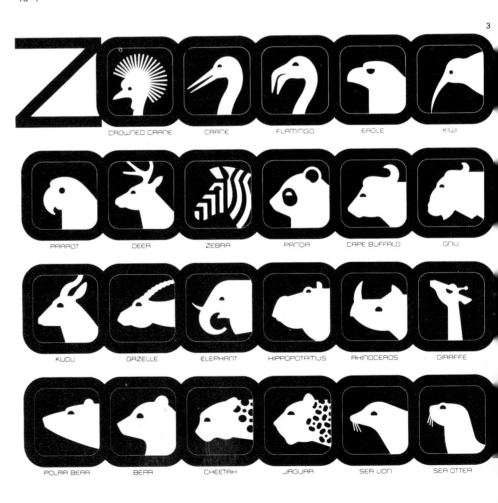

CROWNED CRANE CRANE FLAMINGO EAGLE KIWI

PARROT DEER ZEBRA PANDA CAPE BUFFALO GNU

KUDU GAZELLE ELEPHANT HIPPOPOTAMUS RHINOCEROS GIRAFFE

POLAR BEAR BEAR CHEETAH JAGUAR SEA LION SEA OTTER

2a

2b

2c

4a– c

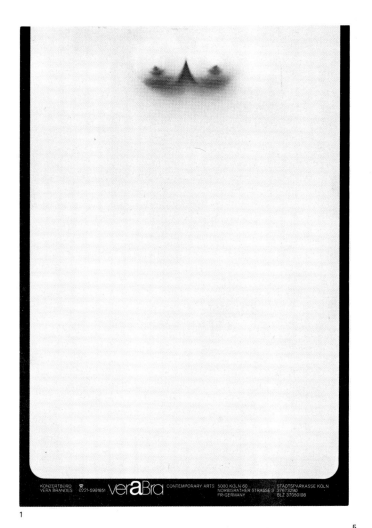

KONZERTBÜRO ☎ 0221-599185I **verABra** CONTEMPORARY ARTS 5000 KÖLN 60 STADTSPARKASSE KÖLN
VERA BRANDES NORBISRATHER STRASSE 3 37673290
FR-GERMANY BLZ 37050198

1

Valerie Kemp
and Michele Beint
represent great
illustrators

To see our portfolio
either call us
at 370 6602
or 373 8917

Freelance
Management
Limited
28 Bramham Gardens
London SW5

2

5

6

Bloomsbury Galleries

Partners-Graeme Reed-Rosemary Murray

16 Bury Place, London WC1 England Tel. 01-831-6539 VAT 234 5227 80

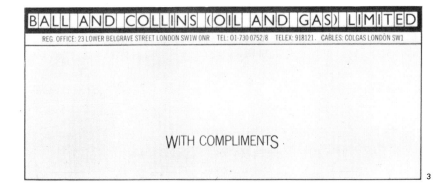

BALL AND COLLINS (OIL AND GAS) LIMITED

REG. OFFICE: 23 LOWER BELGRAVE STREET LONDON SW1W 0NR   TEL: 01-730 0752/8   TELEX: 918121.   CABLES: COLGAS LONDON SW1

WITH COMPLIMENTS .

3

Established 1893

Ferns

Coffee Specialists

L. Fern & Co. Limited
Head Office
27 Rathbone Place
Oxford Street
London W1P 2EP
Telephone 01-636 2237

4

troy

JOSEF TROY + CO
TRANSPORTE
A 6921 HARD VORARLBERG
POSTFACH 18
TELEFON (05574) 33175
BANKVERBINDUNGEN
GENOSSENSCHAFTSVERBAND
BREGENZ KONTO NR. 520971
RAIFFEISENKASSE HARD
KONTO NR. 2904
SPARKASSE BREGENZ
FILIALE HARD KONTO NR. 2044535

7

Wharfe Dale
FILM PRODUCTIONS

11 SALTAIRE ROAD
SHIPLEY YORKSHIRE
TEL. 0274 594407

8

Zillemarkt

Büro:
1 Berlin 12
Giesebrechtstraße 7
Telefon 883 75 16

Zillemarkt GmbH & Co
Gaststätten KG
1 Berlin 12
Bleibtreustraße 48 a

Konto:
Hypo-Bank Berlin 260 0146 443

Zillemarkt, 1 Berlin 12, Bleibtreustraße 48 a.

9

FIGUREHEAD

4 Pont Street London SW1
Tel: 01 235 6360/6248

Chelsea Green Ltd., Registered Office: Farley Court, Allsop Place, London NW1 5LG
Registered in England No. 1188861
Clients private calls 01 235 6346

1

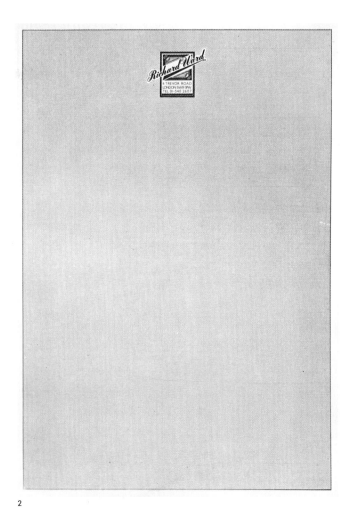

2

5

The Peter Upton Partnership

60 Welbeck Street London W1M 8JN   Tel: 01-584-6232
Partners: Peter J. G. Upton, Patricia A. Upton.

6

FORBES ENTERPRISES (1975) LTD.

74 CARR RD. MT ROSKILL. BOX 5251 AUCKLAND. N.Z. CABLES: HOTSTAMP TELEPHONE 697 153

DETAILS OF ACCOUNT RENDERED			
OVER 2 MONTHS	2 MONTHS	LAST MONTH	BALANCE
DATE INVOICE No.	DEBITS	CREDITS	

FORBES ENTERPRISES (1975) LTD.

74 CARR RD. MT ROSKILL. BOX 5251 AUCKLAND. N.Z. CABLES: HOTSTAMP TELEPHONE 697 153

IS REPRESENTED HERE BY

VICTOR HOPWOOD

3

گروه آزاد فیلم خیابان فرح شمالی شماره ۲۳ – تلفن ۷۵۲۸۹۲ – تهران

4

Manuel Jusdado·Fotógrafo·Bolivia 26
Telf. 458 7807·Madrid 16

7

8

9

1 Great Britain
AD Figurehead
AG Ian Logan Associates
DES Ian Logan
hairdresser, coiffeur, Friseur

2 Great Britain
AD/DES Richard Ward
designer

3 Finland
AD/AG Ateljee Omppu
DIR/DES Osmo Omenamäki
designer

4 Iran
AD Azad Film Group
DES Morteza Momayez
film group

5 Great Britain
AD Peter Upton Partnership
DES Phillip Green
designs for children's bedding, literies
d'enfants, Kinderbettwäsche

6 New Zealand
AD Forbes Enterprises (1975) Ltd
AG Design Link Ltd
DIR Pat Burke
DES S. Moase, T. McLeod
COPY Pat Burke
printing house, imprimerie, Druckerei

7 Spain
AD Manuel Jusdado
DES Fernando Medina
photographer

8 Great Britain
AD The Packaging Company
AG Castle Chappell & Ptners
DIR/DES John B. Castle
ILL Peter Williams
packaging company, emballage, Verpackung

9 Canada
AD Sunnydale Learning Centres
AG Harry Agensky Design
DIR/DES Harry Agensky
educational

1

ROBERT + EBBA BORKOWSKY FOTOGRAFEN

5000 KÖLN-LINDENTHAL ZÜLPICHER STRASSE 355 RUF: 43 69 31
KREISSPARKASSE KÖLN 68408

5

2

6

MR BEETON
AND
MR TENNANT

NUMBER 110
DRAYCOTT AVENUE
CHELSEA
LONDON SW3 3AE

CUSTOMERS
01 589 9120
SUPPLIERS
01 589 9898

charley's   charley's   charley's   charley's   charley's
sport   sport   sport   sport   sport
shop   shop   shop   shop   shop

706 SOUTH LINCOLN
URBANA, ILLINOIS
61801
217/344-6960

20 Middlefield Road
Hoddesdon Herts EN11 9ED
Telephone (61) 63920

3

AKDENİZ TEKSTİL ve MODA FESTİVALİ MERSİN

4

A P Moulds Limited

Victoria Road
Burgess Hill
Sussex RH15 9LF
Telephone Burgess Hill 5333/7
Telegrams Hettich Burgess Hill
Telex 87269

7

Pierrot Publishing Ltd

17 Oakley Road London N1 3LL Tel 01 226 0573

8

9

C	CE	%	÷
7	8	9	x
4	5	6	–
1	2	3	+
0		·	=

Antonio Vittorio Sorge
Finanza e Controllo
Via Principessa Clotilde 7
00196 Roma
Telefono 316487

1 South Africa
AD Exposures
AG Derek Spaull Graphics
DIR/DES Derek Spaull
photographer

2 Germany
AD Robert Borkowsky
DES Heinz Bähr
photographer

3 Great Britain
AD Brian and Patricia Davis
DIR Patricia Davis
DES Brian Davis

4 Turkey
AD The Municipality of Mersin
AG OPA, Organization Marketing Research Co.
DIR Sahin Tekgündüz
DES Bülent Erkmen
textile and Fashion Festival, festival textile et de
la mode

5 Great Britain
AD Mr Beeton, Mr Tennant
AG Pentagram
DIR John McConnell
DES Howard Brown
take-away meals, plats à emporter,
Fertigspeisen

6 United States
AD Charles Schierer
DES Lanny Sommese
athletic equipment

7 Great Britain
AD Hettich
AG Design Research Unit
DIR Christopher Timings
DES Brian M. Dedman
engineering

8 Great Britain
AD Pierrot Publishing
AG Ian Logan Associates
DES Ian Logan
publishing

9 Italy
AD Sorge
AG Promos
DIR/DES Peter Butler
financial group

Packaging

Emballages

Verpackung

1 Great Britain
AD Crabtree & Evelyn
AG Peter Windett Associates
DIR/DES Peter Windett
ILL Caroline Smith
soap packs, savon, Seife

2 Holland
AD Printhouse, Rotterdam
DES Printhouse creative design

3 Great Britain
AD Crysalis Records
AG Shirtsleeve Studio
DIR Malcolm Fowler
ILL Malcolm Fowler, Nancy Fouts
record, plaque de gramophone, Platte

4 Great Britain
AD Harrods
AG Ian Logan Associates
DES Ian Logan
gift packs, emballage pour cadeaux,
Geschenkverpackung

5 Great Britain
AD Pillans & Wilsons
AG James Gardiner Associates
DIR/DES James Gardiner
printer's bicentenary promotion, bi-centenaire
de l'imprimerie, Druckerei Zweihundertjahr
Feier

1

2

3

4

5

1

2

4

5

8

7

3a

3b

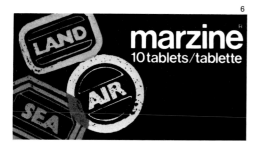

6

1 United States
AD The Nestle Company Inc.
AG Peterson & Blyth Associates Inc.
DIR Ronald A. Peterson
DES Ronald A. Peterson, Steve Hastings
cakemix

2 United States
AD Brown Company
DIR Robert Stoming
DES Brown Company Design Department
flour, farine, Mehl

3a-b Great Britain
AD Beecham Products
AG Cato Johnson Associates
DIR/DES Roger Harris
pharmaceuticals

4 Germany
AD Tchibo Frisch-Röst-Kaffee
DES Peter Schmidt
tins of coffee, boites de café, Kaffee in Dosen

5 Great Britain
AD Park Cake Bakeries
AG Minale, Tattersfield, Provinciali Ltd
cake, gateau, Torte

6 South Africa
AD Wellcome (Pty) Ltd
AG Derek Spaull Graphics
DIR/DES Derek Spaull
pharmaceuticals

7 Australia
AD Robert Timms Pty Ltd
AG Cato Hibberd Hawksby Pty Ltd
coffee, café

8 Denmark
AD FDB (Danish Cooperative Wholesale Soc.)
AG RT
DIR Jørgen Madsen
DES Ingerlill
cornflakes

9 Australia
AD Peters Ice Cream
AG John Clemenger Pty Ltd
DIR Lee Kennedy
DES Cato Hibberd Hawksby Pty Ltd
icecream, crème à la glace, Gefrorenes

9

1

2

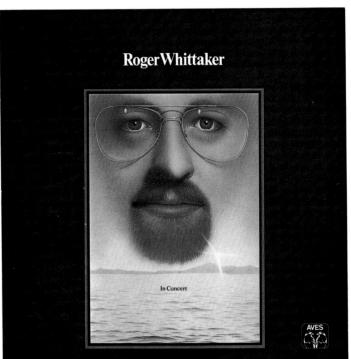

5

6

9

10

3

4

1 Germany
AD/AG Ariola-Eurodisc GmbH
DIR Manfred Vormstein
DES Manfred Vormstein, Annette Krämer

2 Germany
AD/AG Ariola-Eurodisc GmbH
DIR Manfred Vormstein
DES Manfred Vormstein, Matthias Kortemeier

3 Great Britain
AD Music for Pleasure
AG MFP Design Studio
DIR David Wharin
DES Geoff Hocking
children's record, disque pour enfants,
Kinderschallplatte

4 Great Britain
AD Music for Pleasure Ltd
AG MFP Design Studio
DIR David Wharin
DES David Smee
children's record, disque pour enfants

5 Germany
AD Aves Records
DES Peter Schmidt

6 Australia
AD Phonogram Records
AG Graphic Concept
DIR/DES Maurice Schlesinger

7 Switzerland
AD Electromusic S.A.
DES Walter Grieder

8 Germany
AD Vicky Leandros
AG Ideeteam
DIR/DES Peter Brunken

9 Germany
AD/AG Ariola-Eurodisc GmbH
DIR Manfred Vormstein
ILL Mouche Vormstein

10 Germany
AD Deutsche Grammophon
DES Holger Matthies

11 United States
AD Calla
AG P. J. Artists
DES Eli Besalel

12 Great Britain
AD Transatlantic Records
DIR Philip Warr
ILL Lyn Gray, Hat Studio

7

8

11

12

1

2

3

5

SOLCOGRAFT *patch*
SOLCOGRAFT
SOLCOGRAFT
SOLCOGRAFT
SOLCOGRAFT
SOLCOGRAFT

Heterologer Gefässpatch bovinen Ursprungs

Patch hétérologue d'origine bovine

Heterologous patch of bovine origin

5 patches

6/5241

6

ready in three minutes

kitchen ready

ROUND BREADED SHRIMP
NET WT. 16 OZ. (1 LB.)

ready in three minutes

UTTERFLY
BREADED SHRIMP
NET. 16 OZ. (1 LB.)

7

t terrine of duck

terrine de canard en croute

terrine de canard en croute

Cherry Valley Gourmet Foods

p duck pâté with sherry

pâté de canard au xeres

pâté de canard au xeres

Cherry Valley Gourmet Foods

g galantine of duck with vermouth

galantine de canard au vermouth

galantine de canard au vermouth

Cherry Valley Gourmet Foods

1 United States
AD/AG Brown Company
DIR Robert Stoming
DES Brown Company Design Department
paper coffee filters, papiers filtres, Papierfilter

2 Denmark
AD FDB (Danish Cooperative Wholesale Soc.)
AG RT
DIR Jørgen Madsen
DES Nina Benko-Lassen
washing powder, poudre de lessive,
Waschpulver

3 United States
AD Colombian Coffee Federation
AG Peterson & Blyth Associates, Inc.
DIR/DES Ronald A. Peterson
coffee, café

4 Argentina
AD Coqueterias
AG Cannon S.A.C.I.
DIR/DES Jorge Daniel Soler
toilet goods for girls, articles de toilette pour les
filles, Toilettenartikel für Mädchen

5 Switzerland
AD Solco Basel AG
AG Institut Dr. Friesewinkel
DES Maya Stange
pharmaceuticals

6 United States
AD Brown Company
AG Robert Stoming
DES Brown Company Design Department
kitchen-ready shrimps, crevettes, Garnelen

7 Great Britain
AD Cherry Valley Farms Ltd
AG David Harris Consultant Design
DIR/DES David Harris
ILL Sidney Day
frozen foods, surgelé

8 United States
AD William Grant & Sons Inc.
AG Gianninoto Associates
DIR John D. Gianni
ILL J. Kirk Davis
liqueur

1a

1b

3

4

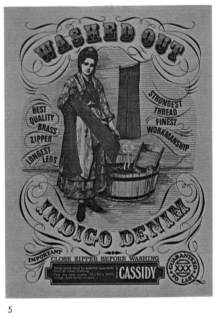

5

6

9

10

2

1

8

12

1a-b United States
AD 7-Up Company
AG Goldsholl Associates
DIR/DES Morton Goldsholl
soft drink, boissons nonàlcooliques,
alkoholfreies Getränk

2 United States
AD The Andrew Jergens Co.
AG Peterson & Blyth Associates Inc.
DIR John S. Blyth
DES John S. Blyth, Steve Hastings
cosmetics

3 Germany
AD Henkel-Khasana
AG Peter Schmidt Studios
DIR Joachim Kellner
deodorant

4 Italy
AD Boy Clan, Harvey Logan
AG Studio Arletti
DIR Ebro Arletti
DES Elis Arletti
jeans

5 South Africa
AD Rex Truform
AG Stilborg & Design
DIR/DES Beni Stilborg
jeans

6 Israel
AD Lodzia
AG A. Degani & E. Kürti
DES Alona Degani, Esther Kürti
shirts, chemises, Hemden

7 Great Britain
AD Rexmore
AG L. A. M. Northwest Ltd
DIR/DES Michel Huey
ILL Mike Monaghan
upholstery fabric, tissu d'ameublement,
Möbelstoffe

8 Great Britain
AD Unicliffe
AG Minale, Tattersfield, Provinciali Ltd
aftershave

9 Germany
AD General Foods GmbH
AG Institut für Packungsgestaltung
DIR/DES Hermann G. Quack
ILL Rolf-Dieter Best
vitamin drink

10 Great Britain
AD Plasplugs
AG The Derek Buchanan Company
DIR/DES Michel H. G. Huet
ILL Geoff Smith
COPY James Denley
plastics

11 Germany
AD Colgate Palmolive Ltd
AG Institut für Packungsgestaltung
DIR/DES Fred Kelber
household cleanser, produit de nettoyage
domestique, Reinigungsmittel

12 India
AD East India Apparel
AG Artcel
DIR/DES Binay Saha
ILL H. Mukherjee
shirts, chemises, Hemden

1a

1b

2

4

5

3a

3b

1a-b Australia
AD Lindemans Wines Pty Ltd
AG Cato Hibberd Hawksby Pty Ltd
wine, vin, Wein

2 Canada
AD Stewart & Morrison
DES Hans Kleefeld
wine, vin, Wein

3a-b Germany
AD Young & Rubicam Advertising, Germany
AG Pentagram
DIR/DES John McConnell
whisky

4 Germany
AD Afri-Cola Bluna GmbH
AG Peter Schmidt Studios
lemonade

5 United States
AD Pepsi-Cola Company
AG Pepsi-Cola Company
DIR/DES Frank Rupp
soft drink, boisson non-alcoolique,
alkoholfreies Getränk

6 Australia
AD Gollin Australia
AG Graphic Concept
DIR/DES Maurice Schlesinger
wine, vin, Wein

7 Great Britain
AD Amalgamated Distilled Products
AG John Harris Design
DIR John Harris
DES Chrissie Button
whisky

8 Germany
AD Illert KG
DES Karl Heinz Franck
liqueur

6

8

7

1

2

4

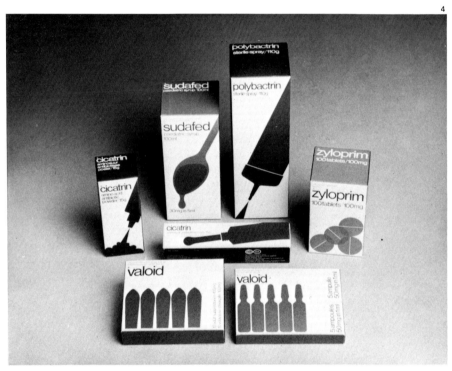

5

6

10 Disposable
Examination Gloves

Anusol

for
haemorrhoids
that hurt

Relieves the irritation and discomfort of haemorrhoids and all anorectal disorders.

Anusol **suppositories** NHS   Anusol HC **suppositories &**
Anusol **ointment** NHS   **ointment.**

7

3

8

1 Australia
AD State Electricity Commission of Victoria
AG Cato Hibberd Hawksby Pty Ltd
ILL Alex Stitt
educational game for use in schools, jeu
éducatif pour écoles, Pädagogisches Spiel für
Schule

2 United States
AD Al's Garage (store)
AG John Follis & Associates
DIR John Follis
DES Wayne Hunt
ILL Scott Slobodian
store packaging of clothing for young people,
emballage de vêtements pour la jeunesse,
Kleiderpackung für die Jugend

3 Australia
AD Warner Lambert
AG Graphic Concept
DIR/DES Maurice Schlesinger
COPY Annmaree Rowan
pharmaceuticals

4 South Africa
AD Calmic Pharmaceuticals
AG Derek Spaull Graphics
DIR/DES Derek Spaull
pharmaceuticals

5 Great Britain
AD Charnos Ltd
AG David Harris Consultants
DIR/DES David Harris
stockings, bas, Strümpfe

6 United States
AD J. C. Penney Co.
AG Robert P. Gersin Associates Inc.
DIR Robert P. Gersin
DES Paul Hanson, Ken Cooke
ILL Melabee M. Miller
Bicentennial music celebration

7 Holland
AD Selecta B.V.
AG Hato
DIR/DES Han V. D. Toorn
toys, jouets, Spielzeug

8 United States
AD 20th Century Glassworks Ltd
DES Alex Steinweiss
glassworks, verrerie, Glashütte

1

2

5

6

7

10

11

3

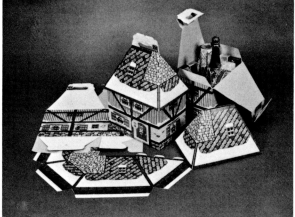

4

8

9

1 Argentina
AD Pibe 'S
AG Cannon S.A.C.I.
DIR/DES Jorge Daniel Soler
toilet goods for children, articles de toilette pour
les petits, Toilettenartikel für Kinder

2 Great Britain
AD Reckitt & Colman
AG Eurographic
sachet for household wipes impregnated with
cleaning solution, sachet pour produits de
nettoyage, Reinigungsmittel

3 Germany
AD Thera GmbH
AG Institut für Packungsgestaltung
DIR Hermann G. Quack
DES Rudi Weiskam
ILL F. C. Gundlach
hair styling

4 Spain
AD Industries Grafiques Duran
AG Estudi Grafic Dis-Art
DIR/DES Toni Vinyes-M. i Gassó
new year's gift, cadeau pour le nouvel an,
Neujahrsgeschenk

5 Australia
AD Yardley Cosmetics
AG Graphic Concept
DIR/DES Maurice Schlesinger
cosmetics

6 Germany
AD Thera GmbH
AG Institut für Packungsgestaltung
DIR Anke-Maria Weber
DES Marion Nass
pharmaceuticals

7 Australia
AD Philip Morris Ltd
AG Cato Hibberd Hawksby Pty Ltd
cigarettes

8 Holland
AD Suiker Unie, Gebroeders van Gilse,
Kandijfabriek B.V.
AG Siedesign
DES Sie Ing Hoat
sugar, sucre, Zucker

9 United States
AD Cosco Chemicals Inc
AG Peterson & Blyth Associates Inc.
DIR Ronald A. Peterson
DES Ronald A. Petersen, Penny Johnson
liquid chemical cleaning and water-softening
products, produits de nettoyage,
Reinigungsmittel

10 Spain
AD Laboratory Abello
AG C.P.A., S.A.
DIR/DES Andrés Puech
tranquilizers for children, calmants pour
enfants, Beruhigungsmittel für Kinder

11 Spain
AD CECSA — compañia electronica y
communicaciones
AG Publicidad Mediterranea
DIR Ramiro Segura
DES Enrique Fernandez
ILL Jose Pallares
COPY Pedro Nagore
radio

12 Germany
AD Mann und Schröder KG
DES Dieter Zembsch
cosmetics

12

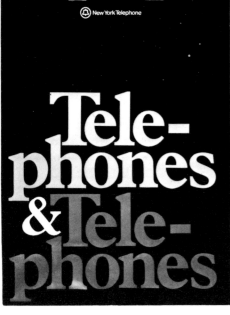

New York Telephone

Tele-phones
&Tele-phones

2

FRAGRANCE IN FASHION
BUSH BOAKE ALLEN

3

circles
with a hole in the middle

REFRAIN Largo Vasto a Chiaia 87 Napoli Tel. 390870

5

6

9

SAINSBURY'S
brilliant white

10

translucently sheer pantyhose $3.00

YVESSAINTLAURENT

SPORTIVO   CACCIATORE   POLITICIZZATO   SEDUTTORE   SPIRITOSO   MAFIOSO   ROMANTICO

NATURALISTA   COLLEZIONISTA   CASALINGO   SPORTIVO   CACCIATORE   POLITICIZZATO   SEDUTTORE

FICCANASO   PROFESSORE   SAXOFONISTA   NATURALISTA   COLLEZIONISTA   CASALINGO   SPORTIVO

io libro di Natale è Mondadori ● ce l'hai un amico

4

1 United States
AD American Telephone & Telegraph
AG Robert P. Gersin Associates Inc.
DIR Louis Nelson
DES Ronald Wong, Paul Hanson
ILL Ronald Wong
telephone retail store

2 Great Britain
AD Bush, Boake, Allen
AG Design Research Unit
DES Richard Dragun
cosmetics

3 Italy
AD Refrain-Record shop
DES Alfredo Profeta
records, disques, Platten

4 Italy
AD Arnoldo Mondadori Editore
Servizio Grafico Editoriale
DIR Arturo Martinez
DES Ferenc Pintér
publisher, editeurs, Verleger

5 Germany
AD Mouson Cosmetic
DES Peter Schmidt Studios
soap, savon, Seife

6 Germany
AD Rollmann & Rose Strumpffabriken
AG Udo Zisowsky
DES Zisowsky Oehring
stockings, bas, Strümpfe

7 Great Britain
AD The Ravenhead Company Ltd
AG Ad Graphics Ltd
DIR Ken Brown
DES Brian Davis
ILL David Lawson
glassware, verrerie, Glas

8 Denmark
AD Superland
AG Mogens Raffel
DIR Sven Scherling, Finn Andersen, Johnny Lund
DES/ILL Johnny Lund
supermarket

9 Great Britain
AD J. Sainsbury Ltd
AG Sainsbury's Design Studio
DIR/DES Peter J. Dixon
emulsion paints, couleurs, Farben

10 United States
AD Kayser Roth Hosiery Co.
AG Robert P. Gersin Associates Inc.
DIR Robert P. Gersin
DES Paul Hanson, Ken Cooke
ILL Paul Hanson
pantyhose, collant, Strumpfose

11 Great Britain
AD Iraqi Dates Organization, Baghdad
AG Eurographic Ltd
fresh dates, dattes, Datteln

12 United States
AD Venture Foods Inc.
AG Robert P. Gersin Associates Inc.
DIR Louis Nelson
DES/ILL Paul Hanson
yoghurt

13 Finland
AD Värmebolagen
AG Paperituote Advertising
DIR Heikki Toivola
DES Osmo Mutanen
barbecue charcoal bag, sac de charbon de bois, Holzkohlensack

7

6 Ravenhead HOBNOBS

6 Ravenhead HOBNOBS
12 oz (34cl)

8

SUPERLAND

11

SINDBAD DATES   SINDBAD DATES

SINDBAD DATES   SINDBAD DATES

13

Grillkol
Värmebolagen
STOCKHOLM OCH YSTAD

12

Screen advertising, Titles
Annonces de l'écran, Titres
Film- und TV-Werbung, Titel

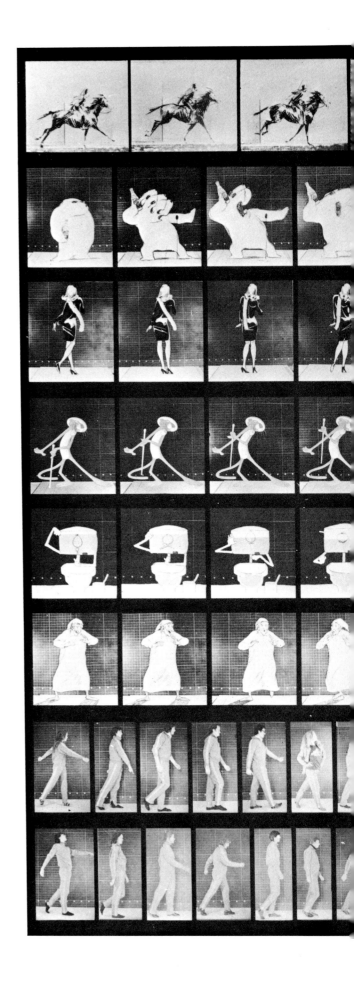

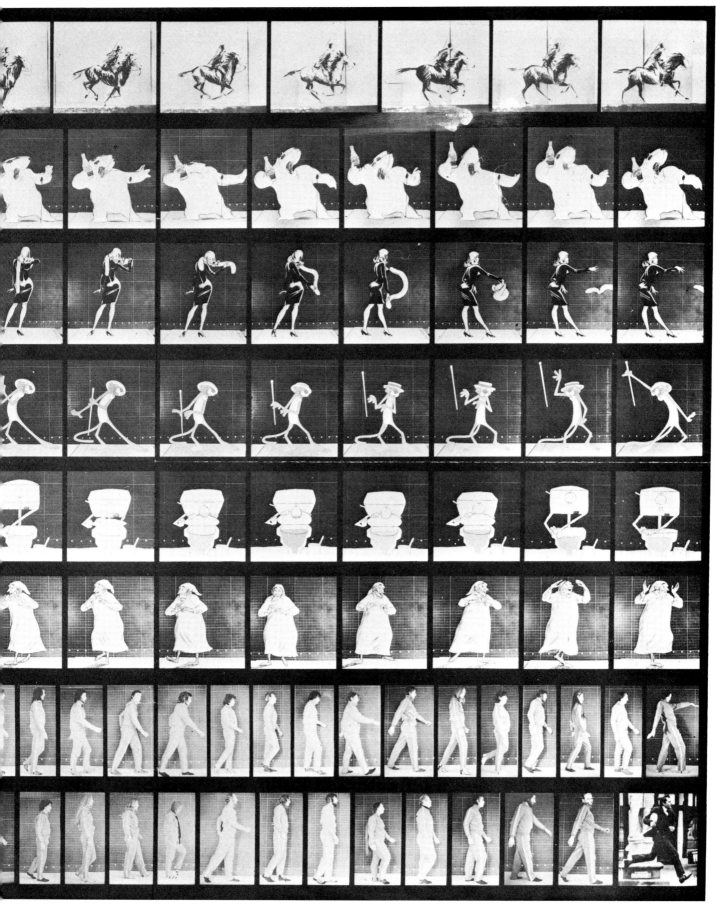

STAFF WALKING: WISHING YOU A MOVING CHRISTMAS AND AN ANIMATED NEW YEAR. FROM ALL AT RICHARD WILLIAMS ANIMATION, 13 SOHO SQUARE, LONDON W.1., ENGLAND.

With apologies to Eadweard Muybridge

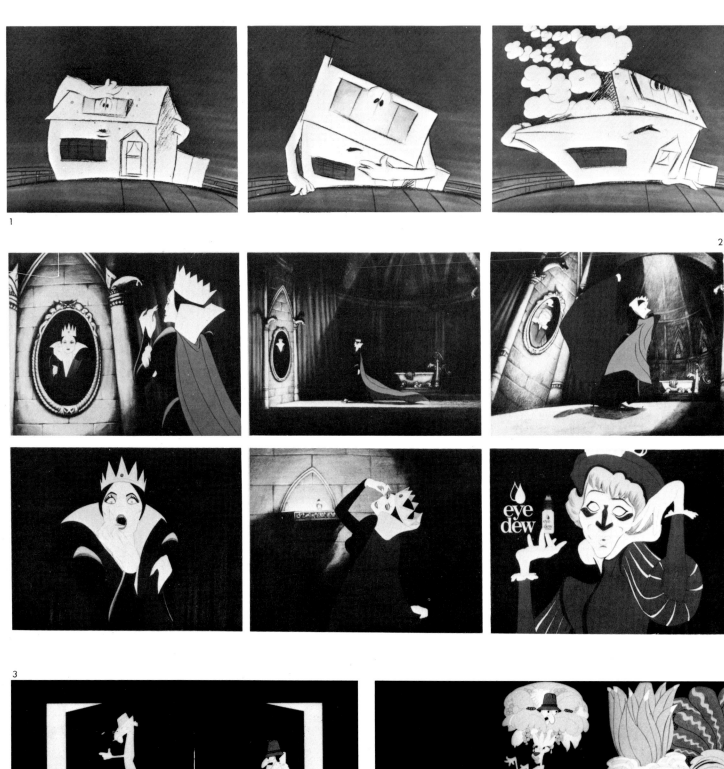

1

2

3

4 a

b

c

d

e

f

g

h

i

j

Screen advertising, Titles
Annonces de l'écran, Titres
Film- und TV-Werbung, Titel

1 Great Britain
AD Department of Energy/C.O.I.
AG Young & Rubicam Ltd
DIR Clive Atkins/Richard Dearing
ILL Richard Williams
COPY Clive Atkins
fuel economy, economie dans l'usage de
combustibles, Sparen von Heizmaterial

2 Great Britain
AD Optrex
AG Davidson, Pearce, Berry & Spottiswoode
ANIMATION DIR Richard Purdum
DES Rowland B. Wilson
ANIMATOR Richard Purdum
COPY David Little
eye drops, gouttes pour les yeux, Augentropfen

3 Great Britain
AD U.A.
DIRECTOR OF LIVE ACTION Blake Edwards
DIR & PRODUCER OF TITLES Richard Williams
PRINCIPAL ANIMATORS Richard Williams, Ken
Harris
film

4a-j Argentine
AD SRT Servicios de Radio y Televisión de la
Universidad de Cordoba
AG Departamento de Diseño de los SRT
DIR/DES Miguel De Lorenzi
ILL (e-j) Oscar Begüan
television titles/promotion slides

1a

1b

1c

**Screen advertising,
Titles
Annonces de l'écran,
Titres
Film- und TV-Werbung,
Titel**

1a-c Italy
AD RAI — Radiotelevisione Italiana
AG Studio Ruffolo
DIR/DES Sergio Ruffolo
opening of television series, début de série de
télévision, Fernseher Serie

2a-b Finland
AD/AG Finnish Broadcasting Company
DIR/DES Tapio Soivio
(a) How to study
(b) Russian language course, cours de langue
russe, Russischer Sprachkurs

2a

2 b

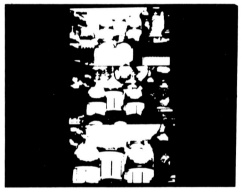

Screen advertising,
Titles
Annonces de l'écran,
Titres
Film- und TV-Werbung,
Titel

1a-b Holland
AD (a) Zanussi Nederland NV
    (b) Bankers F. van Lanschot
AG NPO — Nationale Publiciteits Onderneming
BV
TV DIR Erik de Vries
PRODUCTION Film Group One and Zagreb Film
ILL Nedeljko Dragic
COPY (a) Erik de Vries, (b) Joop Cranendonk
(a) refrigerators, (b) bank

2a-c Great Britain
AD/AG Granada Television Ltd
DIR/DES Keith S. Aldred
children's story series, série de contes
d'enfants, Kindermärchen

3a-c Great Britain
AD BBC
AG (a-c) BBC Television Centre
    (b) BBC Graphic Design Dept
DIR/DES (a) Rosalind Dallas,
        (b) Rosemary Turner,
        (c) Liz Friedman
ILL (a) Rosalind Dallas,
        (c) Paul Johnson
(a) programme on teenage problems,
(b) children's stories from around the world,
contes d'enfants, Kindermärchen
(c) education programmes on economics

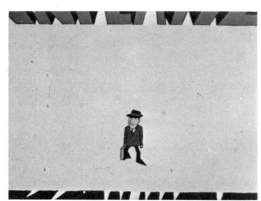
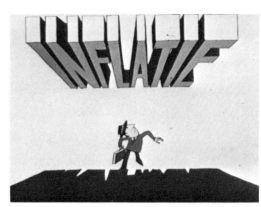

1a

1b

2a

FEBRUARY WEATHER

SEPTEMBER WEATHER

UNTAMED WORLD

3a

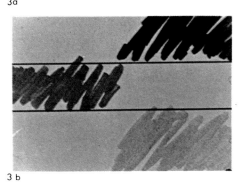
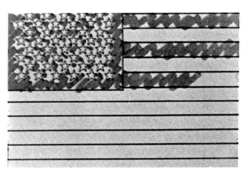

3 b

3 c

2

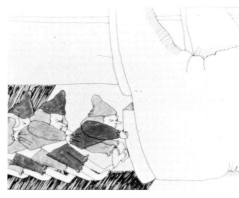

c

2a

2b

Screen advertising, Titles
Annonces de l'écran, Titres
Film- und TV-Werbung, Titel

1a-c Holland
AD Nederlands Zuivelbureau
AG Prad BV
DIR Harry Geelen
RADIO/TV DIR Lous Kouwenberg
PRODUCTION Toonder Studio
SOUNDSTUDIO Cinetone
milk, lait, Milch

2a-f Great Britain
AG Halas & Batchelor
DIR (a) Tony White, (b,c,f) John Halas,
    (d,e) John Halas, Joy Batchelor
DES (b,c) Geoff Dunbar, (f) Stan Hayward
PROD (a) John Halas
(a) quartet
(b) Scroobious Pip
(c) Walrus & Carpenter
(d,e) For Better for Worse
(f) computer

2c

2 d–e

2f

1

2a

b

c

d

e

f

g

h

4

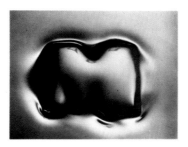

Screen advertising,
Titles
Annonces de l'écran,
Titres
Film- und TV-Werbung,
Titel

1 Holland
AD Zanussi Nederland NV
AG NPO — Nationale Publiciteits Onderneming
TV DIR Erik de Vries
FILM PRODUCTION Film Group One and
Zagreb Film
ILL Nedeljko Dragic, Aleksander Marks
COPY Erik de Vries
freezers for small houses

3a

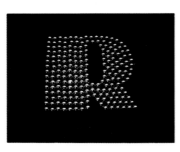

2 (a-h) Great Britain
AD (a) Basel Fair,
(b) Dutch Flower Growers Association,
(c) Mars Galaxy Counters,
(d,g) Golden Wonder,
(e) H. J. Heinz,
(f) The Bristol & West Building Society,
(h) Typhoo Tea
AG (a) Partner Films, Basel,
(b) HVR Advertising Den Haag,
(c,d,g) Masius Wynne Williams & D'Arcy
MacManus,
(e) Dorland Advertising,
(f) Harrison Advertising
(h) Geers Gross Advertising
PRODUCTION Wyatt Cattaneo Productions
DIR (a) Beth McFall, (b) Alison de Vere,
(c,e,f,g) Ron Wyatt, (d,h) Tony Cattaneo
(a) fair
(b) flowers, fleurs, Blumen
(c,d,e,g,h) food, alimentation, Nahrungsmittel
(f) building society, société hypothécaire,
Hypothekengesellschaft

3a-c Great Britain
AD BBC
AG Graphic Design Department, BBC TV Centre
DIR (a) Pauline Talbot, Richard Loncraine,
(b) Alan Jeapes, (c) Ray Ogden
VISUAL EFFECTS DES (a) Ian Scoones
FILM CAMERAMAN (a) Brian Tufano
ILL (b) Michael Sanders,
(c) Graham McCallum, Peter Silk, Bob
Cosford, Glenn Carwithen, Tom Brooks, Ray
Ogden
non-fiction, documentaire

3 b

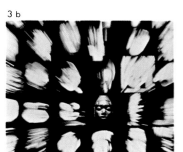

4 Holland
AD N.V. Papierfabriek Gennep
AG Prad B.V.
DIR Geoff Dunbar
RADIO/TV DIR Lous Kouwenberg
PRODUCTION CO Dragon Productions
toilet paper, papier de toilette, Klosettpapier

3 c

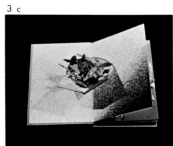

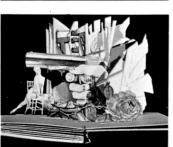

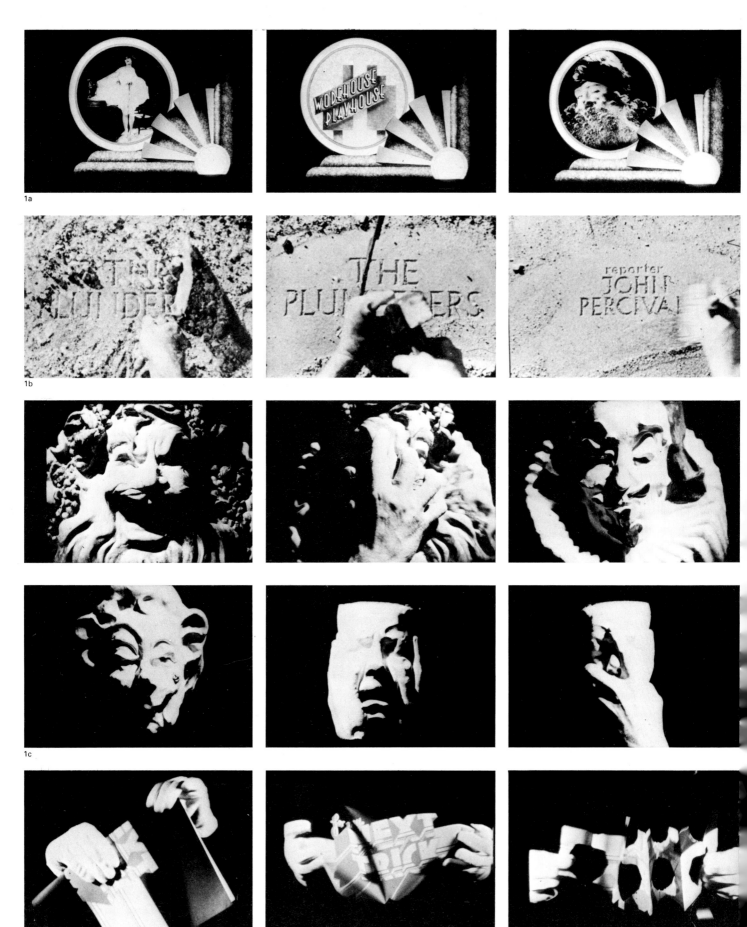

1a

1b

1c

1d

2a

b

c

d

e

f

3a

b

1e

Screen advertising, Titles
Annonces de l'écran, Titres
Film- und TV-Werbung, Titel

1a-e Great Britain
AD BBC
AG BBC Television Centre
DIR/DES (a) Liz Friedman, (b) Sid Sutton,
(c) Stefan Pstrowski,
(d,e) Robert Blagden
ILL (a) Peter Dobie, (d) Mick Brownfield
(a,c,e) drama, (b) documentary series,
(d) children's programme, programme pour
enfants, Kinderprogram

2a-f Great Britain
AD/AG Granada Television
DES Philip Buckley

3a-b Bulgaria
AD/AG Committee for Television and Radio
DES Nikola Petrov Nikolov
(a) non-fiction, documentaire
(b) letters from TV viewers

Direct Mail,
Company reports,
House organs

Brochures,
Rapports annuels,
Journaux d'entreprises

Broschüren,
Jahresberichte,
Hauszeitschriften

1a-j Great Britain
AD Volvo Concessionaires
AG Trickett & Webb Ltd
DIR Lynn Trickett, Brian Webb
DES Lynn Trickett, Brian Webb, Andrew Thomas
motor-car, auto

1a

b

c

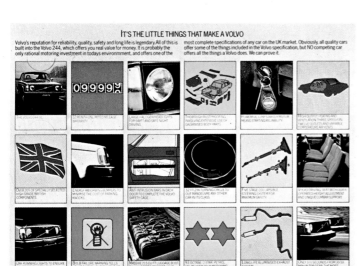

IT'S THE LITTLE THINGS THAT MAKE A VOLVO

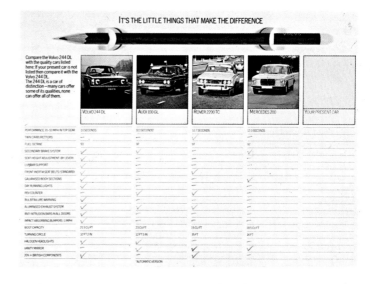

IT'S THE LITTLE THINGS THAT MAKE THE DIFFERENCE

d

The Volvo 264 with its Borg Warner Automatic Gearbox and its 2.7 litre V6 engine proved to be something of a revelation

The Volvo 264 corners as well as any of the higher priced European saloon cars; its suspension soaks up the most rugged Finnish bumps without difficulty and the power steering takes any effort out of driving while still giving an adequate amount of feel. The heating and ventilation system is probably the most impressive for any car.

James Ensor
Financial Times
1st February 1975

Volvo 264
The facts

Sweden's gentle giant

I covered more than 500 miles in less than 24 hours with the 264 and never felt in the slightest fatigued. It says much for the car as the return journey was undertaken minutes after completing an extensive 12-car testing programme at Silverstone involving at least another 200 miles.

David Williams
The Journal, Newcastle upon Tyne
4th June 1975

The Volvo 264 is available with manual or automatic transmission. Both transmissions are new. The gear changing is fast and, in the case of the automatic, virtually unnoticeable – giving excellent acceleration.

The 264's heating and ventilation system is second to none. It is extremely adjustable with numerous outlets inlets both in the front and rear of the car. The 264GL of course has the supreme independence of air conditioning.

e

f

g

The start of something small.

Volvo 66

1

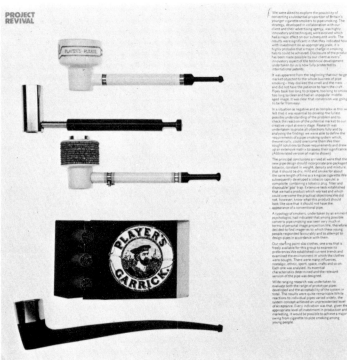

2

4a

b

Américan story.

(1) CARLIN pantalon en jersey jean.
Du 2 au 16 ans. 8 couleurs
DAMY col roulé fin en maille
polyamide Dropnyl Helanca
Du 1 au 16 ans. 12 couleurs
(2) ARKANSAS ensemble pantalon
et marinière jean. 100% coton.
Du 2 au 16 ans. 2 nuances "indigo"
et "jean"
(3) OHIO short jean 100% coton
Du 2 au 16 ans. 2 nuances "indigo"
et "jean"
IOWA tee-shirt en coton. Du 2 au
12 ans. 3 couleurs
(4) TEXAS pantalon jean 100%
coton. Du 2 au 16 ans. 2 nuances
"indigo" et "jean" TOPEKA
chemise version madras en coton
polyosique. Du 2 au 16 ans.
Existe aussi en vichy. 100% coton.

*** best-seller d'Absorba

dropnyl Helanca

1a-b Great Britain
AD Martha Hill Ltd
DES Martha Hill
ILL Mike Martin
outsize fashion

2 Great Britain
AD Sampson/Fether
AG Cope & Davies Ltd
DES Tony Rostron
ILL Mike Nuttala, (photo) Derek Askem, Ian O'Leary
COPY Peter Sampson,
Ben Fether
promotional literature

3 France
AD Absorba
AG Mafia
children's clothing

4a-b United States
AD Euromoney Publications Ltd
DES John Constable
EDITOR Padriac Fallon
financial journal

5a-c Germany
AD Swakara-Team, J. W. Thompson
AG Olaf Leu Design
DIR/DES Olaf Leu, Fritz Hofrichter

6 Great Britain
AD The Armouries, H.M. Tower of London
AG HMSO — Her Majesty's Stationery Office
DIR G. Hammond
DES G. Hammond, S. Mater
ILL Jeremy Hall
COPY Guy Wilson
collection of crossbows, arbaletes, Armbrusten

3

5a-b-c

6

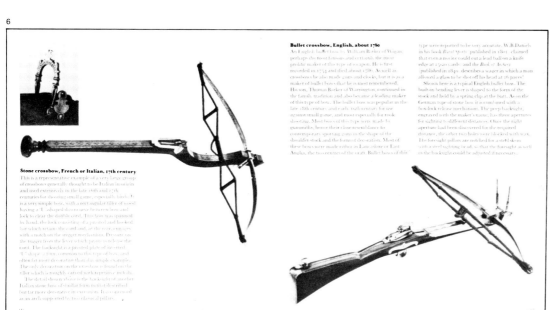

Bullet crossbow, English, about 1780

Stone crossbow, French or Italian, 17th century

Welcome
to the World
Ski Championships
Lahti Finland
1978

1a

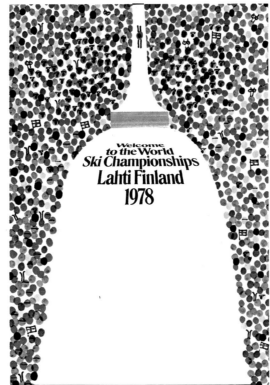

Welcome
to the World
Ski Championships
Lahti Finland
1978

b

78
Welcome to Lahti

c

3a–b

Ski it! See it!
Air Canada's Quebec

Sign up for fun ... in Ontario and Quebec!
Air Canada's Winter Welcome

Bierologie
auf
hessisch.

Grüner Faden
für das zügige Studium eines Bieres,
das mit der Natur aufs herzlichste verwachsen ist.

4a–b

Proprio a Porto Cervo, nella parte ovest
della baie e accanto al porto già esistente,
è stato realizzato uno dei progetti più
importanti e più impegnativi della Costa
Smeralda: la costruzione di una "Marina",
cioè di un porto turistico che offre posti barca
fissi e tutto quello che è necessario ad un
ormeggio permanente.

1a-b Finland
AD World Ski Championships Lahti
AG Mainostoimisto Varis Poteri Veistola Oy
DIR/DES Kyösti Varis
ski championships

2 Italy
AD Costa Smeralda
AG Promos
DIR Bob Elliott
ILL Art Kane
brochure

3a-b United States
AD Air Canada
AG Warwick, Welsh & Miller
DIR/DES George Tscherny
ILL Ivor Sharp
COPY Robert Davidson
tourism

4a-b Germany
AD Licher Bier
AG Ideealismus GmbH
DIR Harald Schlüter
ILL Doris Schlüter, Walter von Deschwanden
COPY Jürgen Mehl
beer

5 Hong Kong
AD The Hongkong and Shanghai Banking Corp.
AG Graphic Communication Ltd
DIR/DES Henry Steiner
ILL Harry Redl, USA
bank, banque

6a-b Denmark
AD Skanderborg Andels Boligforening
AG Weber & Sorensen reklamebureau a/s
DIR/DES Ron Canham
COPY Erik Ansvang
apartments

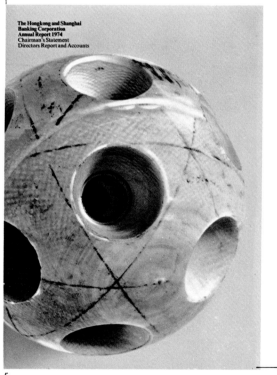

The Hongkong and Shanghai
Banking Corporation
Annual Report 1974
Chairman's Statement
Directors Report and Accounts

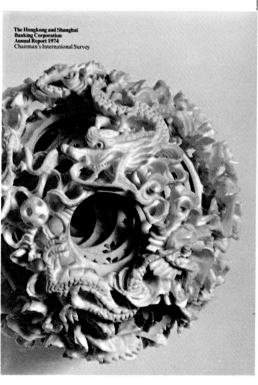

The Hongkong and Shanghai
Banking Corporation
Annual Report 1974
Chairman's International Survey

5

6a

6b

Die Einrichtung
Beringer u. Koettgen
Möbel
Innenausbau
Stoffe
Teppiche
Kunsthandwerk
Leuchten
8 München 2
Brienner Straße 12
und
Wittelsbacher Platz 1
Telefon 23091

Durchgang zu unseren Räumen im ARCO-PALAIS, entlang des roten Läufers, rechts Liege von KNOLL-INTERNATIONAL, mit Spiegeldecke, Lampe Mod. 5077, Teppich mit Blumenmuster in allen Farbkombinationen nach Ihren Wünschen lieferbar.

117

1a-b

2a-b

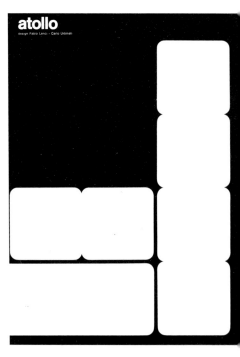

atollo
design Fabio Lenci - Carlo Urbinati

4a-b

IL PICCOLO GATSBY

SE OGGI E' IMPORTANTE L'IMPEGNO RECIPROCO
PER UNA DIVERSA REALTA' DI MERCATO
ALLORA LIDMAN L'IMPEGNO LO DIMOSTRA
INVESTENDO IN PUBBLICITA'
PER UNA LINEA DI SUCCESSO:
"IL PICCOLO GATSBY"
QUINDI ORA IL SUCCESSO E' TUTTO VOSTRO
(E PER TUTTO IL 1975)

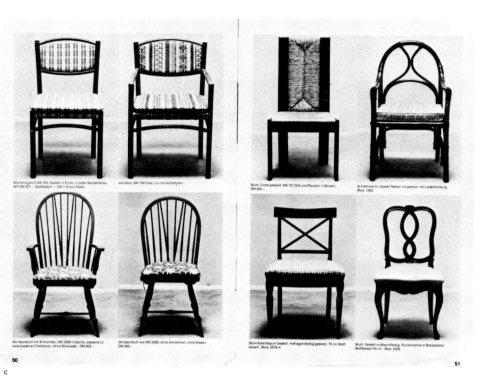

50

51

c

1a-c Germany
AD Die Einrichtung München
AG Apollon
DIR/DES Lutz Roeder
ILL A. Hengstenberg
furniture, meubles, Möbel

2a-b Italy
AD Sleeping System
AG Studio Giob
DIR/DES R. del Sordo, G. Berlinghieri
ILL E. Isaia
folding furniture, meubles pliantes, Faltmöbel

3 Holland
AD 'Artifort' Wagemans & Van Tuinen B.V.
DES Leen Averink
furniture, meubles, Möbel

4a-b Italy
AD Roche, Milano
AG Studioelle
DIR/DES Ennio Lucini
chemicals

3

1a–b

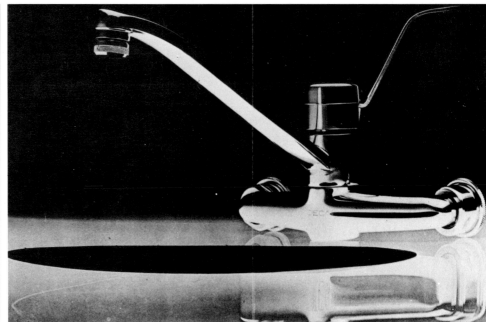

3

Der "Hengstenberger" mit Mildessa Quick.

Im Geschmack einfach herzhaft und delikat! Und so leicht ist dieser Snack zuzubereiten. Sie schneiden ein Brötchen in der Mitte auseinander und rösten beide Hälften knusprig. In einem Topf Mildessa Quick und Wiener Würstchen warm machen. Dann schichten Sie auf die eine Hälfte des Brötchens eine Lage Mildessa Quick von Hengstenberg, die aufgeschnittenen Wiener, ein wenig Delikatess-Senf und noch eine kräftige Lage dampfendes Mildessa Quick. Deckel drauf – fertig ist der Hengstenberger.

Melone mit Mildessa von Hengstenberg.

Mild, erfrischend und leicht ist dieser Salat. Und so wird er gemacht: Rotbackigen Apfel entkernen, in Scheiben schneiden und achteln. Eine Melone oben abschneiden. Kerne entfernen und Melonenfleisch herausschälen. Einen zentimeterdicken Rand stehenlassen. Fruchtfleisch würfeln. Mildessa von Hengstenberg. Apfelscheiben (bis auf einen kleinen Rest zum Verzieren) und Melone vermischen und in die Melonenschale füllen. Esti noch einen Schuß ungesüßte Sahne darübergeben.

Das sind sie – die schmackhaften Feinwürzigen: Kraut von Hengstenberg, Mildessa, Mildessa Quick und Rotessa, die auch den kleinen Imbiß zu einem wahren Leckerbissen machen. Mildessa, das milde Weinsauerkraut und Rotessa, das feingewürzte Rotkraut gibt es jeweils in praktischen Portionsdosen für 2, 4 und 6 Personen. Und Mildessa Quick, das neue, fertig zubereitete Weinsauerkraut von Hengstenberg gibt es in Dosen für 2 und 4 Personen. Mildessa Quick ist kalorienarm (60 kcal je 100 g) und durch viele Zutaten im Geschmack harmonisch abgestimmt.

4

Ein so schöner Bezugsstoff macht einen Sessel zum Thron – finden König Jochen und Königin Ingrid.

1 WK-Möbelstoffe erfüllen in Gewebeausführung und Design-stellt für die höchsten Ansprüche.

2 WK-Möbelstoffe sind auf Druck- und Scheuerfestigkeit geprüft. Sie bieten für jede Polstertechnik und jeden Raum-Ihr richtiges Material: Gleiches Design auf Baumwolle, Leinen oder Velours.

3 WK-Möbelstoffe sind in Farbe und Design auf die 23 Tendenzfarben abgestimmt und harmonieren mit WK-Dekostoffen und WK-Teppichen.

Bezugsstoff: Baumwoll-Velours VENETO aubergine. In 3 weiteren Farbstellungen farbbar: tabac, perla, umbra.

7a–b

FROM ALCAN   A BETTER WINDOW ON THE WORLD

DESIGN PRODUCTS

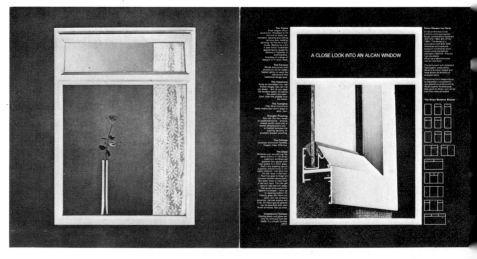

A CLOSE LOOK INTO AN ALCAN WINDOW

DENVER SQUARE—THE SUM OF ITS PARTS

OFFICES
Dominating downtown Denver, the office tower's steel and reflective glass facing will project a sense of strength while possessing a high degree of esthetic value. Thirty nine floors offer more than 20,000 square feet of column-free office space. The airy, multi-level arcade through which access is provided to the tower, contains retail store areas, an open-air restaurant, and banking facilities. Escalators will provide silent, inter-level passage, and the elevator system servicing the tower is engineered for efficient, swift inter-floor movement.

RETAIL STORES
Retail shop areas comprise an integral part of Denver Square's total environment concept. Three levels of skylit space, luxuriously planted and artfully blending outdoors and indoors, will attract consumer traffic to this most modern of market places.

HOTEL
INN ON THE PARK will bring to Denver the gracious hospitality for which the Four Seasons Hotels, Ltd. has gained international reputation. The vertical fluting of the hotel's precast concrete-glass facade, one of the most striking physical features of the Denver Square complex, is actually a carefully engineered feature that provides each room with a view towards the mountains. The hotel's 532 guest rooms will be distinguished by quiet luxury, soft clear lighting and noiseless effective temperature control. Special care has been devoted to produce an elevator system that facilitates effortless movement of guests through the hotel's 26 floors. Tasteful colors and materials, including a lavish use of stone facing, will render the double lobby, with its European bar and giant fireplace, one of the most striking and handsome hotel entrances in the nation.

BALLROOM
A large second-floor ballroom, which will combine old world charm with contemporary decor, has been planned to accommodate large groups in comfortable splendor. Above the ballroom, comprising almost one-quarter of a block, will be a roof garden deck for recreation, sunning and relaxation.

CLUB FACILITIES
The club area, to house the prestigious PETROLEUM CLUB and its dining facilities, will feature an unimpaired panoramic view of Denver and the Rocky Mountains.

2

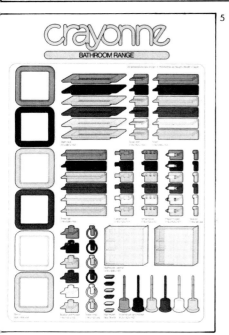

5

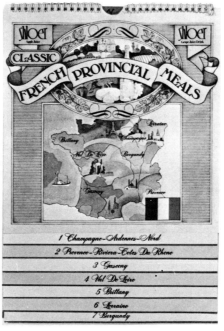

6

8

Greenmarket Tenant's Handbook

9

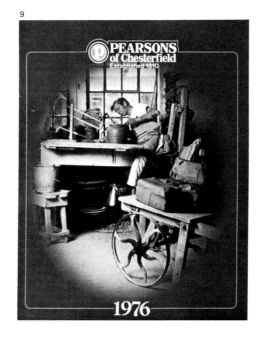

1 Brazil
AD Metais Santiários Deca S.A.
AG DPZ – Dualibi, Petit, Zaragoza
DIR José Zaragoza
ILL Moacyr Lugato
COPY João Augusto Palhares Neto
sanitary appliances, fournitures hygiéniques, Artikel für Hygiene

2 United States
AD Denver Square
AG Wyman & Cannan Company
DIR Lance Wyman, Bill Cannan
DES Lance Wyman, Bill Cannan, Brian Flahive, Tucker Viemeister
ILL Albert Lorenz Studio, (photo) Jack Horner
COPY Bob Slater
brochure

3 Germany
AD Fa. Rich Hengstenberg
AG Apollon
DIR/DES Lutz Roeder
food, aliments, choucroute et chou rouge, Weinsauerkraut u. Rotkraut

4 Germany
AD Wk - Textile
AG Apollon
DIR/DES Lutz Roeder
ILL A. Hengstenberg
furniture, Möbel

5 Great Britain
AD Crayonne Ltd
AG Conran Associates
DIR/DES Stafford Cliff
COPY Alwyn Reynolds
bathroom accessories, articles pour salle-de-bain, Badezimmer-zubehör

6 Great Britain
AD Beecham Products
AG Cato Johnson Associates
DIR/DES Roger Harris
pharmaceuticals

7 Great Britain
AD Alcan Design Products
AG John Nash & Friends
DIR/DES John Nash
ILL George Nicholls
COPY Ian McIness
aluminium windows and doors, fenêtres et portes en aluminium, Aluminium Fenster und Türen

8 Great Britain
AD City of Newcastle upon Tyne
AG Unit Five Design Ltd
DIR Philip Gell
DES Pat Sumner
city market tenant's handbook

9 Great Britain
AD Pearson & Co
AG Ad Graphics
DIR/DES Brian Davis
ILL David Lawson
hand-crafted stoneware

If you want to work the milk run, you'll certainly be well-paid.

Unless you happen to be very rich, the only way you'll ever get to fly an aeroplane on a regular basis is to fly one that belongs to somebody else.

Which means flying for the Air Force.

Or flying for a commercial airline.

We'd be the first to admit commercial airlines have it all over us when it comes to putting cash in your pocket.

We'd also be the first to assert that we do a lot of expensive things that the commercial airlines are unlikely to be able to afford in the next hundred years.

For instance, the airlines want you to clock up 500 hours on a light aircraft before they'll even begin to consider you.

If you've got the money and time, they still won't make any guarantees.

1a–b

If you want to dream about flying, we've got a nice comfortable place for you to do it in.

Point Cook is the home of the RAAF Academy and our first Flying School.

But it's certainly no place like home. Most of the differences will be noticed immediately.

First of all, the average home isn't 18 miles outside Melbourne on the shores of Port Phillip Bay.

So it can't offer the same activities Point Cook can. Like water skiing, speed-boating and yachting.

Point Cook, however, is not all beer and skittles. When you go there, you go to work, to get a degree, to become an officer.

If you're to become an engineer, you'll be there for a year. But if you're to become a pilot, you'll be there for four years.

So you'll be spending a lot of time in our lecture halls and our metallurgical lab, and around our hologram wind tunnel and our neutron monitor.

Once again, you won't have unlimited time here either.

Because when you're not studying your degree course subjects, or helping our staff with their research projects in such areas as flame ions, gamma rays and satellite tracking, we'll expect you to be making sure that our extensive sports facilities aren't going to waste.

You can race your mates around our sports ground. Or race a sea yacht around our bay.

Or try out those water skis that we mentioned earlier.

Or build a radio, a model aeroplane or a supermodified sports car.

If this seems like we're trying to make it sound like heaven, let us be the first to correct ourselves.

Point Cook isn't heaven. It's an Air Force base.

There will be times when it'll drive you crazy and times when you'll want to get away from it all.

So the only realistic thing we can do is help you.

And the simplest way to do that is with a programme of dances, dinners, parties and other social functions which we'll arrange for you both at Point Cook and away from it.

However, for your first few years, we'll have to prevent you from enjoying the one thing you really want: getting your hands on an F111 or anything like it.

But we can't stop you dreaming.

We have it on good authority that the comfortable beds we provide are ideal for just that purpose.

4a–b

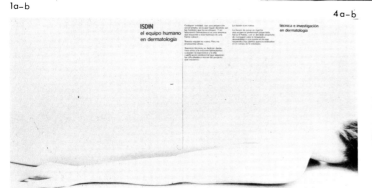

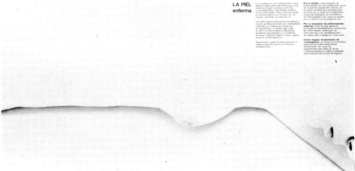

5a

b

6a

6b

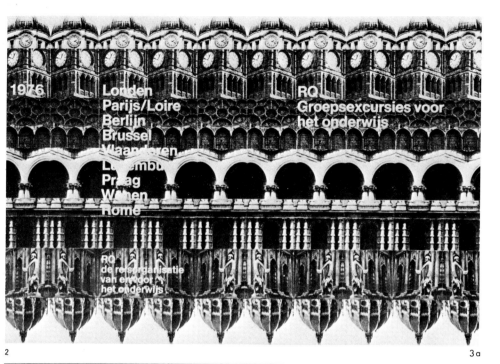

2

3a

3b

Tesco 1973   Legal and General Assurance Society 1974

1a-b Australia
AD A.G.A.S. (Director General of Recruiting)
AG Grey Advertising Australia Pty Ltd
DIR/DES Bart Pavlovich
ILL John Ashenhurst, Tony Stewart, Bruce
Bowers, John Quinn
R.A.A.F. – air force recruiting, recrutement pour
l'aviation, Rekruticrung für Luftwaffe

2 Holland
AD Publiprint
DES Arjen F. de Groot
tourism

3a-b Great Britain
AD (a) Octopus Productions
    (b) Milton Keynes Development Corp.
AG Minale Tattersfield, Provinciali Ltd
(a) pop-up book on conference sets
(b) booklet for offices and industry, information
pour bureaux et industrie, Information für Büro
und Industrie

4a-b Spain
AD Lab. Isdin, S.A.
AG Pharma-Consult, S.A.
DIR/DES Vicente Olmos
ILL Joan Enric, Vicente Olmos
pharmaceuticals

5a-b Italy
AD Gel
AG Perlier S.p.A.
cigars

6a-b Germany
AD Braunschweigisches Landesmuseum
AG Staatliche Hochschule für Bildende Künste
Braunschweig
DIR K. Grözinger, H.-D. Buchwald
DES/COPY Klaus Bliesener
quiz, Rätsel für Kinder

MD designs

SCHNABEL
METALLWERK

⊕BHP 3.75
JOURNAL

5a–b

2

3

JBL Enclosure Information Manual

136A Low Frequency Loudspeaker

LE85 Compression Driver and Horn Assembly

Full Range Loudspeakers

Extended Range Loudspeakers

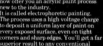

6a–b

CENTURY
A PROFILE
WORTH
KNOWING

We anodise to protect aluminium's natural good looks and to give it a tougher-wearing surface.
Our plant supplies both etched and polished finishes anodised to British Standard specifications.

If you prefer white components, we can now offer you an acrylic paint process new to the industry.
It is called electrophoretic painting. The process uses a high voltage charge to deposit a uniform layer of paint on every exposed surface, even on tight corners and sharp edges. You'll get a far superior result to any conventional spray finish.

The need for close fitting plastic sections within aluminium components carried our expertise into PVC. Today we produce an extensive range of rigid and flexible extrusions. We now supply plastic sections both on their own and in conjunction with aluminium extrusions.

Range of material
PVC rigid tinplates reefs to flexible rubbers.
Standard colours are white, black and grey, but most colours can be achieved if specially ordered.

Type of profile
Simple sizable to complex vacuum sized box sections.
Maximum capacity 150mm wide rigid sections or approx. weight of 1kg per metre. Minimum general wall thickness 1mm for both rigid and flexible sections.

For special applications
Grades of PVC formulated to suit specific applications are available if requirement is equivalent to 500 kgs in weight. This also applies to non-standard colours.

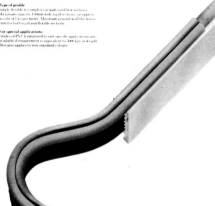

SEMICONDUCTOR
PRODUCT GUIDE '75

TUNGSRAM

4 a–b

guide to
radio and tv
receiving
tubes
'75|76
TUNGSRAM

5 c

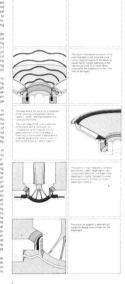

7a-b

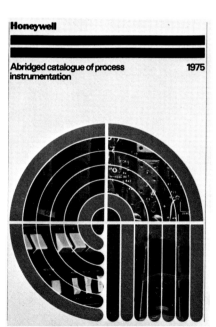

Honeywell

Abridged catalogue of process
instrumentation   1975

Honeywell   EN31-0042

Diffused Silicon Transmitters

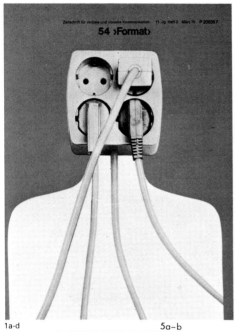

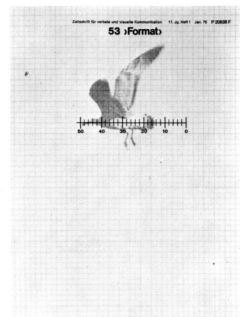

1a–d

5a–b

2

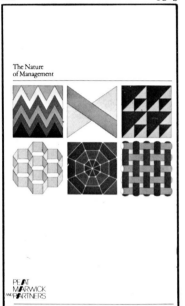

The Nature
of Management

PEAT
MARWICK
AND PARTNERS

If only organizations in human society could function as smoothly as a beehive. But they often don't and that's where we come in. Whenever management suffers from an organizational, personnel or marketing difficulty, Peat, Marwick and Partners are there to help.

Our General Management and Organization services are devoted to identifying and solving overall corporate problems through studies on planning, definition of objectives, profit improvements, economic forecasts, labour relations and management development.

Like a beehive the strength of any organization depends on its workers. Our personnel service can help find them, make them more productive and efficient and ensure their incentive with appropriate salary, compensation and fringe benefits.

To assist in getting goods or services out into the increasingly competitive market place, our Marketing and Economic functions include export market assistance, forecasts, product diversification, pricing, distribution and sales control.

7a–b

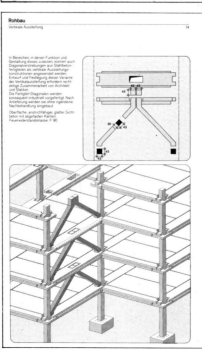

System **elementbau neermoor** Skelettbauten aus Stahlbeton-Fertigteilen

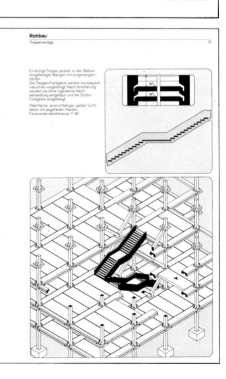

Rohbau
Vertikale Aussteifung   14

In Bereichen, in denen Funktion und Gestaltung dieses zulassen, können auch Diagonalverstrebungen aus Stahlbeton-fertigteilen als vertikale Aussteifungs-konstruktionen angewendet werden. Entwurf und Festlegung dieser Variante der Vertikalaussteifung erfordern recht-zeitige Zusammenarbeit von Architekt und Statiker.
Die Fertigteil-Diagonalen werden konsequent industriell vorgefertigt. Nach Anlieferung werden sie ohne irgendeine Nachbehandlung eingebaut.

Oberfläche, anstrichfähiger, glatter Sicht-beton mit abgefasten Kanten. Feuerwiderstandsklasse: F 90

Rohbau
Treppenanlage   15

Einläufige Treppe parallel zu den Balken. Vorgefertigte Wangen mit eingehängten Stufen.
Die Treppen-Fertigteile werden konsequent industriell vorgefertigt. Nach Anlieferung werden sie ohne irgendeine Nach-behandlung eingebaut und die Stufen-Fertigteile eingehängt.

Oberfläche, anstrichfähiger, glatter Sicht-beton mit abgefasten Kanten. Feuerwiderstandsklasse: F 90

3a-b

4

Direct Mail
Brochures
Broschüren

1a-b Germany
AD Format Zeitschrift für verbale und visuelle Kommunikation
AG Verlag Nadolski Inh. D. Gitzel
DIR Dieter Gitzel
DES (a) Atelier Noth & Hauer
      (b) Schott GmbH Werbeagentur
journal for verbal and visual communication

2 Denmark
AD Nyrup Plastrør
AG Erik Alsing Reklame
DIR/DES Erik Alsing
drainpipes

3a-b Sweden
AD Robert Matton Co AB
AG Atelje Vi Tva
DIR/DES Jan-Ola Åhlström
COPY Lage Ekvall
artists' materials, new address

4 Hungary
AD Museum Budapest
DES János Erdelyi
ILL János Kass
designer's own exhibition

5a-b Canada
AD Peat Marwick & Partners
AG Burns & Cooper Ltd
DIR Robert Burns
DES Dawn Tennant
ILL Mary Ferguson, Freeman Patterson, Barry Ransford, Ruby Watters, C. W. Perkins
4-colour separation
management consultants promotion

6 Denmark
AD Lego System A.S.
AG Horn Reklamebureau
DIR/DES Kay Holm
COPY W. Horn Hansen
construction toy

6a-b

En klods.

Her er historien om den:

En mand fik en idé / Godt legetøj og børns skabertrang. Legetøj med idé og sammenhæng / LEGO® = Leg godt. Fremtid i plastic √ LEGO klodsen / Fra land til land. Atter nye eksperimenter / Voksne er ikke gode til at lege. Leg er barnets arbejde / Børnenes udvikling skaber behov. Skabertrangen / Løse opgaver / Behov for anerkendelse. Kontaktbehov / Skabe i fællesskab / LEGO for alle børn. Mulighederne utallige / LEGO er, hvad børnene gør det til. En ny succes: LEGOLAND® / Store modeller / Miljøer. Udstillinger / Aktiviteter.

LEGO

mange voksne mener, men trangen til at lære tingene at kende og forstå deres opbygning og funktioner.

Med LEGO får børnene afløb for denne lyst uden at gøre skade på noget. Det er simpelthen en del af ideen med LEGO, at man skal bryde ned, hvad man har bygget op – for så at kunne bygge op igen.

Behovet for at bruge sig selv er vigtigt for barnets fysiske udvikling. Beherskelse af bevægelser er en forudsætning for en lang række færdigheder, væsentlige for barnets udvikling. LEGO tilfredsstiller i høj grad dette såkaldte motoriske behov, især finmotorikken, d.v.s. fingre og hænder. Og koordination mellem øjne og hænder.

For lidt større børn er det også fundamentalt at løse opgaver. Resultaterne er ofte – set med voksnes øjne – ret ubehjælpsomme, men tilfredsstiller barnet selv, fordi dets fantasi overgår dets kritiske evne.

Børnene får en elementær tilfredsstillelse ved at bygge op og nå frem til et resultat, og denne tilfredsstillelse er ikke blot forbundet med LEGO's universalæsker, men også med modelæskerne. For stoltheden over at løse en opgave, stillet af andre, er ikke mindre, end hvis børnene selv stiller sig en opgave.

Dette hører sammen med det behov for anerkendelse, som er vigtigt for børnenes sunde udvikling. Og netop LEGO giver gennem materialets form, farver og anvendelighed mulighed for ægte anerkendelse fra de voksne. En anerkendelse, som stimulerer barnet.

Herigennem dækkes også det kontaktbehov, som barnet – ligesom alle vi andre – nærer, endda stærkere end de voksne.

Børnepsykologer er enige om, at mange børn, også ubevidst, anvender LEGO som en kontaktmulighed over for forældrene.

For større børn tilfredsstilles kontaktbehovet også gennem de muligheder, LEGO rummer for at lege sammen og skabe noget i fællesskab. Dette at præge noget fælles, men også at tage hensyn til andre er et vigtigt punkt i udviklingen mod at blive en god borger i samfundet – i det store fællesskab.

LEGO er for alle børn. For alle børn kan få noget ud af at lege med LEGO – uanset udviklingstrin.

Og LEGO er også universel i sin idé. Dette kan aflæses af, at LEGO er accepteret over hele verden: Behovsgrundlaget er det samme. Uanset forskellige kulturer og vekslende samfundsformer skal børn have dækket deres behov for at udvikle sig. I denne proces indgår legen som et vigtigt middel – og dermed også LEGO.

For LEGO er ikke kun en ting, men alt, hvad børnene gør det til. I en sjov og spændende verden – i leg med LEGO.

8

Financial Times Industrial Architecture Award 1975

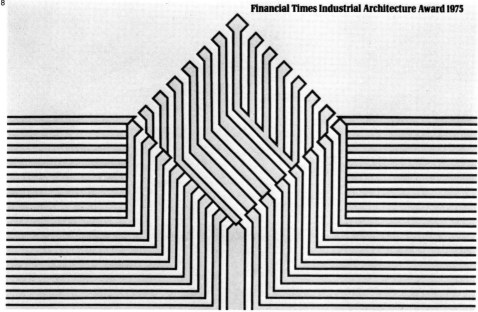

1a–b

2

4 a–b

5

3a–b–c

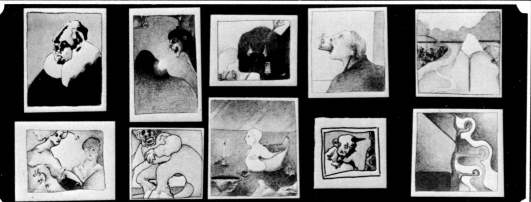

6

1a-b Great Britain
AD Boosey & Hawkes (Music publishers)
AG Pentagram
DIR/DES Mervyn Kurlansky
music — scores and instruments
musique — partitions et instruments
Musik — Partituren und Instrumente

2 Holland
AD Stichting Kunstzinnige Vorming
AG Integral Design Unit
DES Jeanne and Robert Schaap
ILL Jeanne Schaap
cultural magazine for young people,
publication pour la jeunesse, Jugendmagazin

3a-c Great Britain
AD/AG Heinemann Educational Books
DIR/DES Tony Stocks
publisher's catalogues

4a-b United States
AD Herbich & Held
AG Richard Hess Inc.
DIR/DES Richard Hess
promotion for printing company,
imprimerie, Druckerei

5 Germany
AD Leisure Pleasure
AG SSM — Schlüter Schürmann Mehl
tourism

6 Germany
AD Studiotheater (Gunnar Holm-Petersen)
DES Hermann Ludwig
play for children,
theatre pour enfants, Kindertheater

7 Germany
AD Verwaltung der Burgen und Schlösser des
Landes Hessen
AG Grafik-Design-Kraft
tourism

8 Israel
AD Askar Ltd
AG O.K. Advertising Ltd
DIR/DES Abe Rosenfeld
paints, couleurs, Farben

7

8

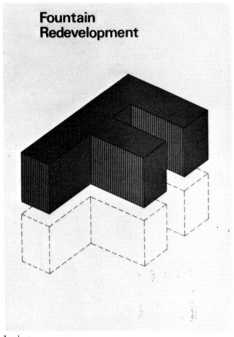

Fountain
Redevelopment

1a–b

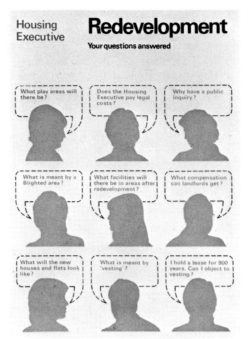

Housing
Executive

Redevelopment
Your questions answered

What play areas will there be ?

Does the Housing Executive pay legal costs ?

Why have a public inquiry ?

What is meant by a Blighted area ?

What facilities will there be in areas after redevelopment ?

What compensation can landlords get ?

What will the new houses and flats look like ?

What is meant by 'vesting' ?

I hold a lease for 900 years. Can I object to vesting ?

Pepsi-Cola

WORLD

2

Annual Report 1974–1975   Rapport annuel 1974–1975

5

Shopping development, Huddersfield   Centre commercial, Huddersfield   Einkaufszentrum, Huddersfield

Architects   **Architectes**   **Architekten**

Main Contractor   **Entreprise de construction principale**   **Hauptunternehmer**

Window Contract Value   **Valeur du contrat de fenêtres**   **Fenster vertragswert**

6

8

vær aktiv

ta' et kursus i AOF

9

A Centre for Humanistic Studies and Organizational Leadership   The Niagara Institute

10

Gödecke AG · Berlin

1. Folge
einer Informationsserie
über Synapsen, Neurotransmitter und Rezeptoren

„Der Endknopf"
und die physiologische Wirkung von
Novadral®

The Canada Council Art Bank Catalogue | Conseil des Arts du Canada Catalogue de la Banque d'oeuvres d'art | September 1972 to March 1975 | Septembre 1972 à Mars 1975

3

immigration to canada

1900-75

4

7a–b

KAMMERMUSIK

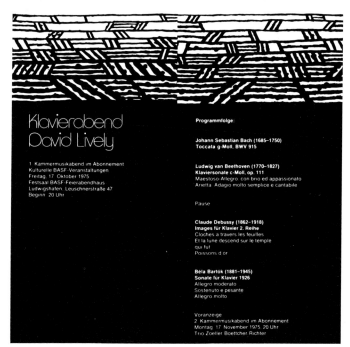

Klavierabend
David Lively

1. Kammermusikabend im Abonnement
Kulturelle BASF-Veranstaltungen
Freitag, 17. Oktober 1975
Festsaal BASF-Feierabendhaus
Ludwigshafen, Leuschnerstraße 47
Beginn 20 Uhr

Programmfolge:

Johann Sebastian Bach (1685–1750)
Toccata g-Moll, BWV 915

Ludwig van Beethoven (1770–1827)
Klaviersonate c-Moll, op. 111
Maestoso-Allegro con brio ed appassionato
Arietta. Adagio molto semplice e cantabile

Pause

Claude Debussy (1862–1918)
Images für Klavier 2. Reihe
Cloches a travers les feuilles
Et la lune descend sur le temple
qui fut
Poissons d'or

Béla Bartók (1881–1945)
Sonate für Klavier 1926
Allegro moderato
Sostenuto e pesante
Allegro molto

Voranzeige
2. Kammermusikabend im Abonnement
Montag, 17. November 1975, 20 Uhr
Trio Zoeller Boettcher-Richter

11a–b

NOVO
DICIONÁRIO
AURÉLIO

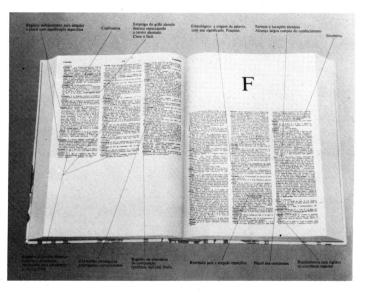

Direct Mail
Brochures
Broschüren

1a-b Great Britain
AD Northern Ireland Housing Executive
AG N.I.H.E. Graphics Unit
DIR Alan Livingston
DES Rodney Millar
redevelopment information

2 United States
AD/AG Pepsi-Cola Company
DIR/DES Bruce James Duhan
COPY Dave G. Houser
soft drink, boissons non-alcooliques,
Alkoholfreie getränke

3 Canada
AD Government of Canada
AG Design Collaborative
DIR/DES Ernst Roch
immigration

4 Canada
AD Canada Council
AG Burton Kramer Assoc. Ltd
DIR Burton Kramer
DES Reinhold Schieber
art bank, banque d'oeuvres d'art, Kunstbank

5 Canada
AD Department of Indian and Northern Affairs
AG Design Collaborative
DIR Rold Harder, Eric Plummer
DES Ernst Roch, Rolf Harder
annual report

6 Great Britain
AD Turner-Fain Ltd
AG John Nash & Friends Ltd
DIR/DES John Nash
ILL Ken Randell
COPY John Hindle
company produce

7a-b Germany
AD BASF Aktiengesellschaft
AG Abteilung AOA/Grafisches Büro
DES Franzi Krause
concert

8 Denmark
AD/AG Lund Hansen/Reklame
DIR Paul Anker
DES Jytte
ILL Ellegaard
COPY Poul Lund Hansen
advertising agency

9 Canada
AD The Niagara Institute
AG Burton Kramer Associates Ltd
DIR Burton Kramer
DES Tim Nielsen
centre for humanistic studies

10 Germany
AD Gödecke AG Berlin
AG Werbeagenture Selinka
DIR/DES Friedemann Hett
pharmaceuticals

11a-b Brazil
AD Editora Nova Fronteira
AG Casa do Desenho
DIR Gian Calvi,
DES Gian Calvi, Antonio Vaz, Raul Rangel
ILL Dick Welton
dictionary

1a–b

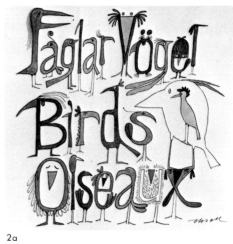

2a

3a–b

2 b–c

4a– c

1a-b Germany
AD Thalia Theater
AG Holger Matthies
DES H. Masalone
theatre

2a-c Sweden
AD/AG Olle Eksell
designer — self-promotion

3a-b United States
AD Monadnock Paper Co.
AG George Tscherny, Inc.
DIR/DES George Tscherny
paper

4a-c Germany
AD Sozialdemokratische Partei Deutschlands
AG Are Kommunikation
DES Helmut Schmid
(a-b) campaign to help the blind, campagne
pour l'aide des aveugles, Blindenwohlfahrt
(c) serial publication of the SDP

5 United States
AD San Jose Symphony Orchestra
AG Sam Smidt Associates
DIR Sam Smidt
DES Sam Smidt, Bob Sleeper
ILL Bob Sleeper
symphony orchestra

5

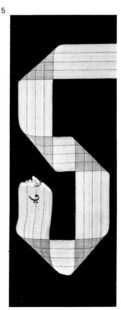

Package Lexikon 90

Contenuti

Modulo 1: sound book
- argomentazioni commerciali

Modulo 2: sound book
- demostrazione standard
- uso del materiale promozionale

Modulo 3: tavola di confronto
- concorrenza

Altro materiale:
Sales guide: guida figurata
- riepilogo delle argomentazioni, per la presentazione ai clienti

Testi dei moduli 1 e 2:
- cassette registrate (2)
- edizione a stampa

Durata

Modulo 1: 1 h. ca
Modulo 2: 2 h. ca
Modulo 3: consultazione

Package Lexikon 90

Contenu

Module 1: sound book
- arguments commerciaux

Module 2: sound book
- demonstration standard
- usage du materiel promotionnel

Module 3: planches de comparaison
- concurrence

Autre materiel:
Sales guide: guide d'figuré
- resumé des argumentations pour la presentation aux clients

Textes de modules 1 - 2:
- cassettes enregistrées (2)
- imprimés

Durée

Module 1: 1 h.
Module 2: 2 h.
Module 3: consultations

Package Lexikon 90

Contains

Module 1: sound book
- selling points

Module 2: sound book
- standard demonstration
- use of promotional material

Module 3: Chart for Comparison
- competition

Other material:
Sales guide: illustrated guide
- summary of selling points involved in a customer sales presentation

Texts of Modules 1 and 2:
- recorded cassettes (2)
- audio script

Time required

Module 1: about 1 hour
Module 2: about 2 hours
Module 3: for consultation

2a-b

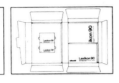

Modulo 1

Argomentazioni commerciali

Obiettivi
Al termine del periodo i partecipanti:
- sanno esporre le argomentazioni commerciali di base: prestazioni esclusive, vantaggi della lesina e della cartuccia intercambiabili, qualità di scrittura, sicurezza, completezza della macchina, ergonomia (simboli nella prima figura)
- sono in grado di sostenere le argomentazioni con le relative prestazioni della macchina (seconda figura: argomentazione - sicurezza - altra figura - prestazioni a sostegno - disattivazioni, bloccaggi, selezioni di sicurezza)

Module 1

Arguments commerciaux

Objectifs
A la fin du cours les élèves:
- doivent savoir exprimer les argumentations commerciales de base: prestations exclusives, avantages de la bobine d'écriture et de la cartouche interchangeables, qualité d'écriture, sécurité, totalité des services, ergonomie (symboles dans la première planche)
- sont en mesure de soutenir les argumentations aidés par les prestations de la machine (deuxième planche, argumentation - sécurité - autres planches, prestations - remouillages, blocages, sélections de sécurité)

Module 1

Selling points

Objectives:
By the end of the module the participants will be able to:
- list the basic selling points: exclusive features, special advantages of the interchangeable printing element and cartridge, printing quality, error protection, complete range of capabilities, ergonomic symbols in the first illustration;
- support the selling points showing the pertinent capabilities of the machine (second illustration: the selling point is - error protection; other illustrations supporting machine capabilities: de-activation, anti-jamming, anti-error controls)

Sound book

È un sistema audiovisivo composto da:

Un set di tavole illustrate, raccolte in un volume, che visualizzano, con figure e simboli, un argomento didattico.
- Poiché è esclusa ogni parola scritta, il set può essere utilizzato in ogni paese, senza limiti di lingua.
- Il set può restare all'allievo come audiovisivo personale per il richiamo successivo dei nozioni apprese.

Un commento alle tavole registrato su cassetta. Il commento fornisce anche le istruzioni sull'uso del materiale, chiama i partecipanti agli autocontrolli, rinvia, se del caso, ad esercitazioni pratiche sulle macchine.
- L'unico strumento richiesto per l'istruzione con il - Sound Book - è quindi un comune lettore di cassette.

Quando l'istruzione è indirizzata alla pratica sui prodotti nel sistema si inseriscono anche le macchine interessate.
- La prima tavola di ciascun volume indica, con immagini, il materiale e le macchine da predisporre per lo svolgimento del periodo.

L'istruzione può svolgersi individualmente o in gruppo, non è richiesto l'intervento dell'istruttore, poiché il materiale è in autoistruzione.
- Il - Sound Book - può essere utilizzato sia nell'addestramento residenziale che nell'addestramento decentrato.

Sound book

C'est un système audiovisuel composé:

D'un set de planches illustrées, regroupées dans un volume, qui illustrent, grâce à des figures et des symboles, un sujet d'enseignement.
- Le set ne comportant aucun mot écrit, celui-ci peut servir dans tous les pays, évitant ainsi le problème des langues.
- Le set peut être gardé par l'élève comme audiovisuel personnel pour le rappel futur des notions apprises.

D'un commentaire du volume enregistré sur bande magnétique. Le commentaire fournit aussi le mode d'emploi du materiel, invite les participants aux auto-contrôles et renvoit, si nécessaire, à des exercices pratiques sur les machines.
- Le seul instrument nécessaire pour apprendre à l'aide du - Sound Book - est donc un simple lecteur de cassettes.

Quand l'instruction est orientée sur la mise en pratique des produits, le système comprend également les machines intéressées.
- La première planche de chaque volume montre, grâce à des illustrations, le materiel et les machines qu'il faut prévoir pour le déroulement de la période.

L'instruction peut se faire individuellement ou en groupe; l'intervention d'un instructeur n'est pas nécessaire puisque le materiel est en auto-instruction.
- Le - Sound Book - peut être utilisé soit pour l'entraînement au centre de formation soit pour l'entraînement dans les succursales.

Sound book

Is an audio-visual system consisting of:

A set of illustrated plates contained in a single book, which utilizes pictures and symbols to teach a particular aspect.
- Since the written word has been excluded, the set completely overcomes the language barrier and can be used in any country.
- The set can be kept by the salesman as a personal audio-visual medium for reviewing the ideas learned.

A commentary of the pages is recorded on cassette tapes. The commentary also gives instructions regarding the use of material, it defines the participants to make use of the self-testing system, and if necessary it advises practice with the machine.
- The only instrument required for audio-visual instruction with the - Sound Book - is a common cassette player.

When the instruction concerns practice with the products, the respective machines should also be available.
- The first page in each book indicates or pictures language the material and machine required to prepare for each teaching period.

Instruction can be given either singly or in groups. There is no need for an instructor because the material is self-instruction material.
- The sound book can be used both for in-plant and residential training.

1a
1b

7a-b

Lexikon 90

olivetti

Servizio Centrale Formazione Addestramento Commerciale
Centro Formazione Firenze

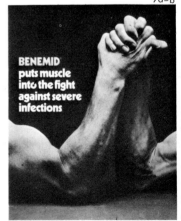

...le viaduc de calix

3

4

OPETUS- JA SIVISTYSTOIMINTA

terveyden - ja sairaanhoito

SOSIAALISET TEHTÄVÄT

6

RAILWAYS
1825
1975

1a-b Italy
AD Olivetti
AG Linke-Bossi
DIR Ornella-Linke-Bossi
COPY Gianni Geronimi
electric typewriters, machines à ecrire
éléctriques, elektrische Schreibmaschinen

2a-b Israel
AD The Plaza Hotel
AG/DES Alona Degani, Esther Kurti
menu covers and placemats for coffee houses,
menus et sous assiettes, Menu und
Tellerunterlagen

3 France
AD Coignet, S.A.
ILL Denise Bourbonnais
construction firm

4 Finland
AD Valkeakoski Town Administration
DIR/DES Heikki Toivola
information booklet on rates, information sur
contributions, Steuerberatung

5 Denmark
AD Roed-Sørensen Leasing
AG Benton & Bowles
DIR John Andersen
ILL Per Koblegaard
COPY Ole Krogh

6 Great Britain
AD The Post Office
AG David Harris Consultant Design
DES David Harris
ILL Brian Cracker
railway centenary stamp pack and brochure,
publicité pour timbres de poste,
Briefmarkenreklame

7a-b Great Britain
AD/AG Merck Sharp & Dohme Ltd
pharmaceuticals

Direct Mail
Brochures
Broschüren

1a-b Australia
AD Vega Press Pty Ltd
AG Cato Hibberd Hawksby Pty Ltd
ILL Ray Condon, Ian Dalton, Alex Stitt
COPY David Webster
printing

2a-c Germany
AD Bayerischer Rundfunk, München
DIR Walter Tafelmaier
DES Michael Tafelmaier, Helmut Bauer
radio programme

3a-b Canada
AD Abitibi Provincial Paper
AG Burns & Cooper Ltd
DIR Robert Burns
DES Roger Hill
ILL Heather Cooper, Paul Walker
newspaper

4a-d Germany
AD Zanders Feinpapiers GmbH
AG Olaf Leu Design
DIR/DES Olaf Leu, Fritz Hofrichter
paper

1a

b

3a

b

Technischer Bericht

Finanzbericht

Sommer 75

2a–b–c

4 a

Chromolux-Wandzier

b

Chromolux-Raubtier

c

Chromolux-Engel

d

Chromolux-Bäng-el

1a–b

Haldol in Delusional Mania
• Has produced calmness and control of agitated delusional behaviour, such as delusions of persecution, imminent danger, and being "talked about",— within 24 hours in hospitalized patients.
• Has proven superior in control of violent symptomatology to chlorpromazine, previously used in the same patients for the same indication.
• Facilitates a quicker release from hospital, due to the calmness, awareness, and normalized thought process of the patient. This becomes highly significant in patients with family responsibilities.

Haldol Initially / Haldol Long Term
• At onset of treatment, HALDOL acts promptly, calming the hostile and highly agitated patient within hours, when time is crucial to all concerned.
• As therapy progresses, even unco-operative, suspicious patients can receive the benefits of HALDOL, since its colorless, odorless, tasteless, *drop* form can be concealed in food or drink.
• The transition from hospital to home and societal environments is facilitated for the paranoid patient, knowing that his manic episodes can be controlled on maintenance HALDOL therapy. Oversedation is not a problem with HALDOL.

PARTICIPE DA CERTEZA DO AMANHÃ

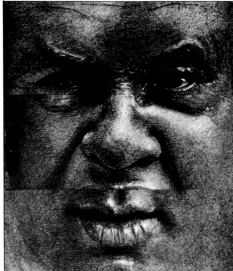

Por exemplo: em caso de aposentadoria, a pessoa continua a receber integralmente o salário, como se estivesse trabalhando.

4a-b

6

7

International Pacific Securities Company, Limited
Annual Report 1975

NIPPON
HONG KONG
SINGAPORE
MALAYSIA
PILIPINAS
AUSTRALIA

The Hongkong and Shanghai Hotels Limited

ANNUAL REPORT '74

2

3

5

8

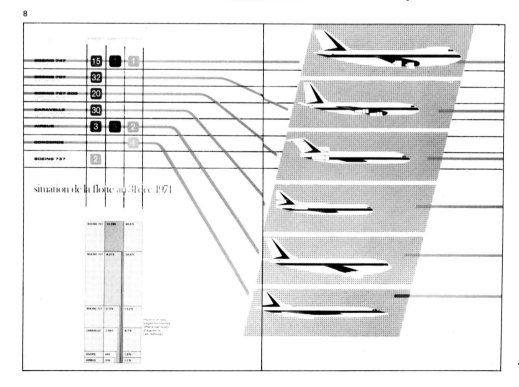

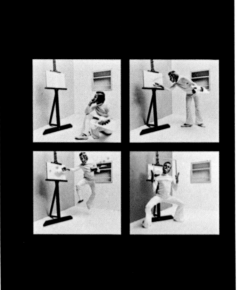

The Company

Standard Brands Paint Company's primary line of business is the retailing of paint, wallcoverings, carpeting and other home decorating products.

Since its inception in 1939, the Company has pioneered the concept of selling products to individuals who work on their own projects and during the ensuing 36 years, this catering to the needs of the "do-it yourselfer" has helped the Company to become one of the leading mass merchandisers in the ever growing home decorating market.

As of September 30, 1975, Standard Brands Paint Company owned and operated 59 retail centers located in Arizona, California, New Mexico, Oregon, Texas and Washington. In addition, the Company owned offices, warehousing and manufacturing facilities in Torrance, California and warehousing and office space in Kent, Washington. Our manufacturing division, Major Paint and Varnish Company produced 75 different lines of paint and paint products, all of which were sold only in the Company outlets. They also produced a complete line of artist colors and mediums for Shiva, Inc. These products were distributed nationally and could be purchased at retail outlets throughout the United States and Canada. Shiva, Inc.'s sales to unaffiliated companies accounted for less than 1% of the Company's total sales.

At the end of our fiscal year 1975, the Company's payroll consisted of 2,287 employees; of these employees, 1,621 were employed at the retail level, while the balance of 666 employees were engaged in manufacturing and various other support activities.

Retail Paint and Decorating Centers

The company's 59 retail paint and decorating centers are bright, colorful, spacious structures that are, for the most part, located on well known boulevards in major shopping areas and have ample free parking adjacent to each store. Because of the company's specialization in the home decorating field, it is possible for the stores to offer an unusual depth of selection in quantities that are large enough to complete most projects.

The centers fall into two basic size categories. Stores in the first category average 11,000 square feet of retailing space and could generally be considered our standard sized outlet. Centers in the second category, of which there are currently 19, are somewhat larger, averaging 16,000 square feet of retail selling space per location. The additional square footage in these larger locations has been utilized to house a greatly expanded carpet section.

In every phase of our store operations, the concentrated emphasis on customer service is apparent. Since most of our customers have little technical knowledge in the home decorating field, "do-it-yourself" experts staff each store and are available to wait on every customer. Their expertise enables them to offer professional advice on any problem arising from a customer's particular decorating project.

Customers

The vast majority of Standard Brands Paint Company's customers are individuals who, for financial reasons and/or personal satisfaction, prefer to do their own home decorating and maintenance. They are of all ages and from all walks of life, brought together by the promise of cost savings and the feeling of pride in their accomplishments. Continually rising professional labor costs, combined with inflationary pressures have encouraged more and more persons to use their leisure time to work on their own projects. The "do-it yourselfer" demands large selections, professional sales

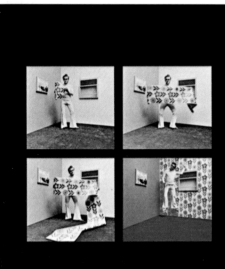

prices have become prohibitive, or are in short supply. They also research raw materials and new products and continually test competitors' products in a never-ending effort toward improving the quality of our paint lines.

Advertising

Standard Brands Paint Company spends approximately 3% of gross sales on advertising and sales promotion, the majority of which is directed toward print advertising and point of purchase display. The program is aimed at effectively reflecting the quality, variety and cost savings available in a Standard Brands Paint and decorating center. During the year, a chainwide television advertising campaign marked the Company's first major entrance into the use of broadcast media. The program was highly successful and plans for the coming year include further involvement in this area. The Company's advertising is handled internally to ensure the dedication and interest needed for successful campaigns and to afford the savings available to the in house advertising agency.

Transportation and Warehousing

Warehousing has long been an important factor in the success of our Company. Our ability to purchase and store unusually large quantities of goods has enabled us to obtain some merchandise in amounts larger than most other companies might want to handle, thereby realizing substantial economies. In addition, we have been able to maintain a year-round flow of imported items which normally require long purchase lead times and in many cases we have been able to offset either shortages or price increases by our ability to "stock up".

Each retail paint and decorating center receives merchandise on a weekly basis. The centers transmit their order via data phone equipment directly to our main office computer facility. Here, the order is resequenced into the same progression of sections that the warehouse merchandise is in, and the warehouse staff, using this "picking" list, fills the order. Once the store's needs are filled, the order is returned to the computer for store billing and inventory control.

Shipments to the stores are made by either a company owned truck or by a contract carrier. The bulk of these deliveries are made by our company owned fleet of 22 tractors and 42 semitrailers. Over 120 loads are shipped per week with a total weight in excess of 5,000,000 pounds.

With the exception of Washington and Oregon, all of the Companies shipping and receiving is done from our central warehousing facilities located in Torrance, California. The six Northwest decorating centers are serviced by our 60,000 square foot warehouse in Kent, Washington. As of September 30, 1975, we had 678,931 square feet of warehousing space under roof.

Facilities

At the end of fiscal 1975, Standard Brands Paint Company occupied a total of 876,171 square feet of modern, fully sprinkler and alarm system protected manufacturing, warehousing, and office space. Of this amount, 816,171 square feet were located on 32 acres of land in Torrance, California, and 60,000 square feet were located on 4 acres of land in Kent, Washington.

The retail store space amounted to 735,079 square feet with adjacent parking for 4,859 automobiles. The Company owns all of its retail stores, warehousing, manufacturing plants and offices, and all of the land on which they are situated. This ownership not only provides for a lower occupancy cost but also eliminates costly lease renegotiation and allows us maximum flexibility regarding relocation or enlargement decisions.

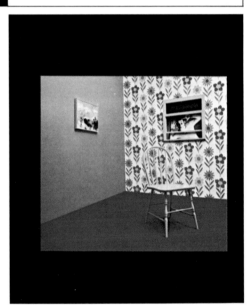

1 a-d

5a-b-c

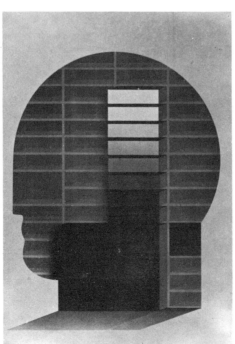

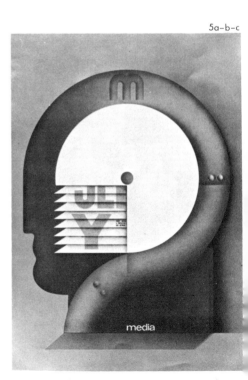

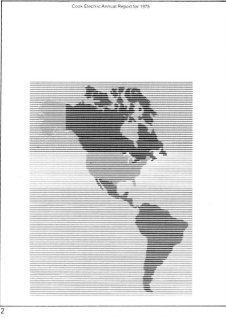

1a-d United States
AD Standard Brands Paint Company
AG The Weller Institute
DIR/DES Don Weller
ILL Roger Marshutz
COPY Sheldon Weinstein
annual report

2 United States
AD Cook Electric Company
AG Edward Hughes Design
DIR/DES Edward Hughes
ILL Joseph Sterling
annual report

3 United States
AD Applied Materials, Inc.
AG Dennis S. Juett & Associates
DIR/DES Dennis S. Juett
ILL Dan Hanrahan
COPY Tom Groener
annual report

4a-b United States
AD Tiger Corporation
AG Robert Miles Runyan & Associates
DIR Robert Miles Runyan
DES Rusty Kay
COPY Steve Benoff
annual report

5a-c Germany
AD MD Papierfabriken
AG Werbeabteilung
ILL Reiner Stolte
annual report

6 United States
AD Winklevoss & Associates
AG Hamoor Communications
DIR/DES Joe Scorsone
COPY Barry Hampe
actuarial consultant

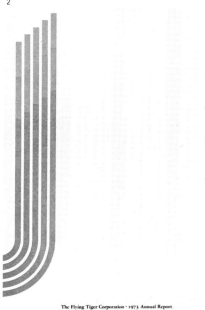

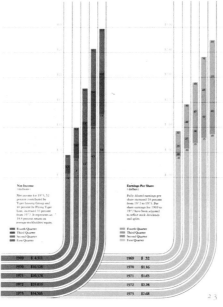

4a–b

6

1a-b-c

3a-b

Biode 1976
Products for health and vitality
Biode Pharmaceutical Industries Ltd Mile 10¼ Ikorodu Rd Lagos Telephone 31642/3

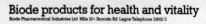

1976	January				February					March			
Sunday		4	11	18	25	1	8	15	22	29		7	14	21	28
Monday		5	12	19	26	2	9	16	23		1	8	15	22	29
Tuesday		6	13	20	27	3	10	17	24		2	9	16	23	30
Wednesday		7	14	21	28	4	11	18	25		3	10	17	24	31
Thursday	1	8	15	22	29	5	12	19	26		4	11	18	25
Friday	2	9	16	23	30	6	13	20	27		5	12	19	26
Saturday	3	10	17	24	31	7	14	21	28		6	13	20	27

Biode products for health and vitality
Biode Pharmaceutical Industries Ltd Mile 10¼ Ikorodu Rd Lagos Telephone 31642/3

2a

d

**Greetings cards,
calendars
Cartes de voeux,
calendriers
Glückwunschkarten,
Kalender**

1a-c Germany
AD Hornauer Verlag
ILL Roger Blachon

2a-b Germany
AD Wilhelm Kumm Verlag
DES (a) Adolf Bernd
     (b) Giovanni Mardersteig, Florence
'Scriptura' — calendar

3a-b Great Britain
AD Biode Pharmaceuticals Ltd
AG Lock/Pettersen Ltd
DIR/DES Glenn Tutssel
ILL Terry Morgan
pharmaceuticals

4a-b Holland
AD Drukkerij Reclame
AG Loridan Studios, Leiden
calendar for printers, calendrier pour
imprimeurs, Kalender für Druckerei

4a

JANUARI						
Z	M	D	W	D	V	Z
				1	2	3
4	5	6	7	8	9	10
11	12	13	14	15	16	17
18	19	20	21	22	23	24
25	26	27	28	29	30	31

b

AUGUSTUS						
Z	M	D	W	D	V	Z
1	2	3	4	5	6	7
8	9	10	11	12	13	14
15	16	17	18	19	20	21
22	23	24	25	26	27	28
29	30	31				

1a–b

2c

3

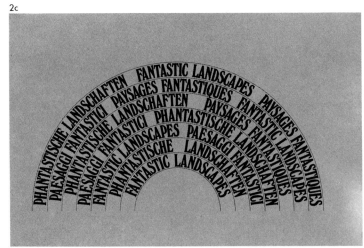

4

1 2 3 4 5 6 7 8 9 10 11 12 13 14 15 16 17 18 19 20 21 22 23 24 25 26 27 28 29 30

Greetings cards, calendars
Cartes de voeux, calendriers
Glückwunschkarten, Kalender

1a-b Germany
AD/AG Eberhard Bauer
DES Ursula Weckherlin
ILL Thomas Lüttge
calendar for machinery manufacturer

2a-c Germany
AD Zanders Papiere
DIR/DES Albrecht Ade
COPY Ade, Rundholz
paper and cardboard, calendar

3 Germany
AD Roland offsetmaschinenfabrik
AG Olaf Leu Design
DIR/DES Olaf Leu, Fritz Hofrichter
ILL Josse Goffin, Belgium
calendar

4 Hungary
AD Budavox Telecommunication Foreign
Trading Company Ltd
AG V.T. Publicity
DIR Mrs S. Zupán
DES L. Görög
ILL Karoly Gink
telecommunications products — calendar

2a–b

1 2 3 4 5 6 7 8 9 10 11 12 13 14 15 16 17 18 19 20 21 22 23 24 25 26 27 28 29 30

1a-b-c

4

תשל"ד - תשל"ה 1974

5

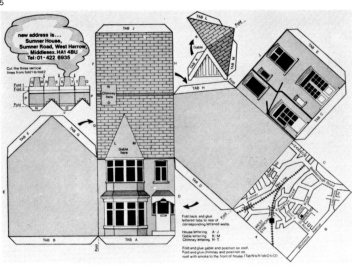

7

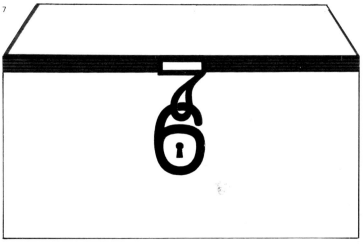

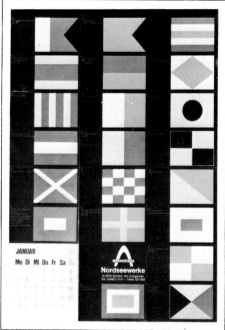

2

3

6a-b

Photographs: Clay Perry, Liam White, Godfrey August
Design: BT Publicity Services Department
Printing: The Kynoch Press England

DEC76

1 2 3 4 5 6 7 8 9 10 11 12 13 14 15 16 17 18 19 20 21 22 23 24 25 26 27 28 29 30 31

2

1a—b

5a—b

K+E-Druckfarbenkalender 76
K+E Printing Ink Calendar 76
Encres d'Imprimerie Calendrier K+E 76

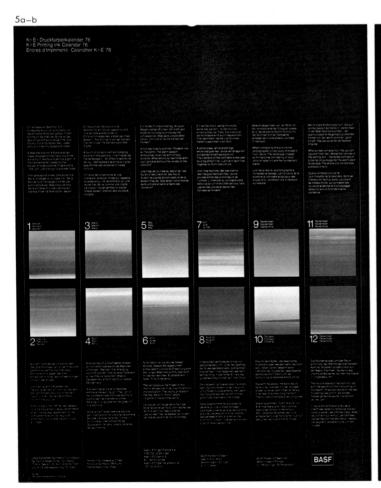

BASF

K+E

February
Sunday	1	8	15	22	29
Monday	2	9	16	23	1
Tuesday	3	10	17	24	2
Wednesday	4	11	18	25	3
Thursday	5	12	19	26	4
Friday	6	13	20	27	5
Saturday	7	14	21	28	6

August
Sunday	1	8	15	22	29
Monday	2	9	16	23	30
Tuesday	3	10	17	24	31
Wednesday	4	11	18	25	1
Thursday	5	12	19	26	2
Friday	6	13	20	27	3
Saturday	7	14	21	28	4

3a–b

4

Greetings cards, calendars
Cartes de voeux, calendriers
Glückwunschkarten, Kalender

1a-b Great Britain
AD ICI London
AG ICI Publicity Services Department
ILL Clay Perry, Liam White, Godfrey Argent
calendar for chemical company

2 Malaysia
AD Borneo Motors (Malaysia) Sdn. Bhd.
AG Ogilvy & Mather (Malaysia) Sdn. Bhd.
DIR/DES Kok Hong Kung
motors

3a-b Great Britain
AD Union Carbide UK Ltd
AG Lock/Pettersen Ltd
DIR/DES Glenn Tutssel, David Lock
COPY Tony Douglas
calendar

4 Brazil
AD/AG Aroldo Araujo Propaganda
DIR/DES Antonio Vaz
self-promotion

5a-b Germany
AD Kast & Ehinger
AG Kast & Ehinger Werbeabteilung
DES Gerhard A. Rosenlöcher
ILL Lajos Keresztes
COPY Dr. Wolfgang Strache

6a-b Italy
AD Olivetti
DES Bruno Bassi

6a–b

1a-d

5

HAPPY NEW YEAR ★ JOHN FOLLIS & ASSOCIATES

6

9

8

3

4

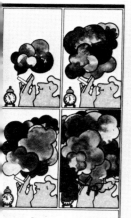

10

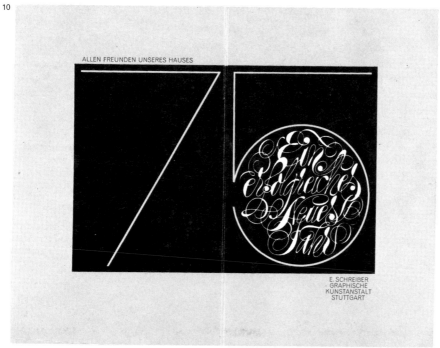

Direct Mail
Brochures
Broschüren

1a-d Holland
AD I.D. Unit
AG Integral Design Unit
DES Jeanne & Robert Schaap
New Year greeting

2 Great Britain
AD Interoute Ltd
AG John Nash & Friends
DIR John Nash
DES Tony Chalcroft, John Nash
ILL Malcolm Smith
Christmas card for international transport
company

3 Denmark
AD Lego system
AG Horn Reklamebureau/Kommunikation
DIR/DES Kay Holm
ILL Grønbeck
New Year card

4a-b Great Britain
AD/DES Malcolm White, David Wharin
Christmas card

5 Great Britain
AD Goldenlay Ltd
DIR Alan Cracknell
DES Roger Harris
deep freezer calendar

6 Hungary
AD Medimpex
ILL Gabriella Hajnal
pharmaceuticals, calendar

1 a – d

2

3

4 a–b

5

6